CHILDHOOD IN CHINA

THE AMERICAN DELEGATION ON EARLY CHILDHOOD DEVELOPMENT IN THE PEOPLE'S REPUBLIC OF CHINA

William Kessen, Chairman

Urie Bronfenbrenner, Bettye Caldwell, John A. Clausen, Alex de Angelis, Jerome Kagan, Eleanor E. Maccoby, George A. Miller, Harold W. Stevenson, Jeannette G. Stone, Martin K. Whyte, Joe Wray, Marian Radke Yarrow

CHILDHOOD IN CHINA

Edited by William Kessen

Yale University Press, New Haven and London

Originally published with assistance from
the Louis Stern Memorial Fund.

Library of Congress catalog card number: 75-8151

International standard book number: 0-300-01910-6 (cloth)
0-300-01917-3 (paper)

Designed by Sally Sullivan

and set in Times Roman type.

Printed in the United States of America by

Alpine Press, South Braintree, Massachusetts

Published in Great Britain, Europe, and Africa by
Yale University Press, Ltd., London.
Distributed in Latin America by Kaiman & Polon,
Inc., New York City; in Australasia by Book & Film
Services, Artarmon, N.S.W., Australia;
in Japan by John Weatherhill, Inc., Tokyo.

CONTENTS

PREPARATION OF THE REPORT

Shortly after our return to the United States, we shared our notes and prepared draft reports on several aspects of our observations. Every member of the delegation participated in the preparation of the report; the ascriptions shown below for particular chapters mark responsibility for assembling and structuring the work of others. All of the report was edited into its final form by William Kessen.

Chapter 1. Initially prepared by Alex de Angelis and Martin K. Whyte.

Chapter 2. Sections initially prepared by Urie Bronfenbrenner, John A. Clausen, and Martin K. Whyte; assembled by Urie Bronfenbrenner.

Chapter 3. Initially prepared by Jerome Kagan, revised by Jeanette G. Stone and Jerome Kagan.

Chapter 4. Initially prepared by Urie Bronfenbrenner, Bettye Caldwell, Harold W. Stevenson, and Jeanette G. Stone; assembled by Bettye Caldwell.

Chapter 5. Initially prepared by Eleanor E. Maccoby.

Chapter 6. Initially prepared by Marian Radke Yarrow, revised by Eleanor E. Maccoby and Martin K. Whyte.

Chapter 7. Initially prepared by George A. Miller.

Chapter 8. Initially prepared by Joe Wray.

PREFACE

In China now there are 127 million primary school students, ten times the number before Liberation; there are 35 million students in middle schools, thirty times the number before Liberation. Only about ten percent of children of primary-school age do not attend school, mostly the children of mountain herdsmen. We must solve this problem.

We have a huge population, a varied population, and we have followed the policy of "walking on two legs" in education. That is, we have schools run by the state and schools run collectively by communes or by neighborhoods. We also advocate different kinds of schools to meet varied needs—morning schools, noon schools, and so on.

Before the Cultural Revolution, our education was interfered with by the revisionist line of Liu Shao-ch'i. Mao Tse-tung's directives had not been carried out and school was rather long—six years of primary, six years of middle school, and four to six years at the university. In day-to-day teaching, bookish knowledge was one-sidedly stressed. Education was divorced from production, practice, and politics. Mao Tse-tung criticized this policy; after so many years in school, students still did not know how peasants grow grain and how workers work in factories or how commodities are exchanged.

The first step after the Cultural Revolution was to shorten the period of school—primary to five years, middle to four or five (after experimentation, we have concluded that five is best), university to three years for the time being. Nineteen seventy-three is the first year of graduation from the three-year university. We must see from the results whether that period is good or not.

Our second step was to change the system of education radically. In schools at all different levels, not only must the students study culture and intellectual knowledge, they must also learn from the workers, peasants, and soldiers. To achieve this purpose, schools set up factories or move into the countryside. Camping is the chief way in which students learn from the People's Liberation Army.

Our aim is to criticize the bourgeoisie, to repudiate bourgeois thinking and the revisionism of Liu Shao-ch'i and Lin Piao. There are two contradictions: between people and enemy and between people and people. Therefore, middle-school graduates do not go directly to the universities; they must do physical labor in a factory or on a farm first. Most do farm work. Universities enroll students from communes and factories after the students have done at least two years of labor. Through this program we will change the system that divorces students from practice, politics, and physical labor. Now we have favorable conditions because we have smashed the revisionist line of Liu Shao-ch'i and the working-class leadership has been strengthened. We are still in the experimental stage, with hardships and obstacles ahead, but we believe we have the correct orientation and we will adhere to this policy.

—Remarks of Hsiao Ching-jo to the American Delegation on Early
Childhood Development, Peking, November 22, 1973

The thirteen members of the American delegation went to China late in 1973 under the auspices of the Committee on Scholarly Communication with the People's Republic of China, a group jointly sponsored by the National Academy of Sciences, the American Council of Learned Societies, and the Social Science Research Council. The delegation on early childhood was the second American group to go to China as a consequence of the Committee's negotiations in Peking in the spring of 1973. We met, both in Peking and Shanghai, the delegation on art and archeology that had preceded us by a few days. We entered China from Hong Kong on November 15, 1973, and departed through Hong Kong on December 5; during our study of child rearing and early education, we traveled from Canton (Kwangchow) to Peking, Sian, Shanghai, and back to Canton. Our official hosts in China were the Education Circles of Peking working through the offices of the Group on Science and Education of the State Council. Mr. Hsieh Ch'i-kang of the Group on Science and Education, and Mr. Hao Shuang-hsing, of the Peking Education Bureau, acted as coordinators and counselors throughout our visit. In each city, translators were provided from the faculties of foreign language institutes.

Our group consisted of eight psychologists, two sociologists, a nursery school teacher, a pediatrician, and a staff member of the Committee on Scholarly Communication; two members of the delegation read and spoke Chinese. We visited seven nurseries, thirteen kindergartens, five primary schools, and three middle schools, as well as hospitals, health clinics, and the Shanghai Youth Palace. We talked with Chinese families in their homes. Of the twenty-eight schools we saw, ten were administered on a city or district level, five were administered by communes, eight by factories, and five by neighborhoods.

The affiliations of the Americans in the delegation, a list of places we visited, and the names of some of our Chinese hosts and informants appear in the last pages of this report.

We were interested in all aspects of child rearing and child care, from the prenatal period through adolescence, but unfortunately the name of our group in literal Chinese was "Kindergartener Education Group," a fact of translation that led to our seeing as many kindergartens as all other levels of school combined. We quickly and somewhat forcefully told our hosts about the much broader scope of our interests and they, with remarkably efficiency, made it possible for us to observe children at all ages short of the university, though still with a heavy emphasis on children between three and six.

A typical visit to a school involved a brief introduction by the principal or responsible person, a tour of the classrooms and play-grounds, a brief look at workshops where students are trained in productive labor, a song and dance performance by the children, and a discussion or question and answer period at the end. In addition to these local discussions held at each school, however, we also had several major discussions with educationists and officials in Peking, with parents, and, in Shanghai, with Little Red Soldiers and Little Red Soldier leaders, kindergarten and normal school teachers, psychologists, and doctors in family planning.

We were eager to see children in rural settings and in places other than the major coastal cities. Our itinerary at first called for us to visit Nanking, but our hosts generously acceded to our request to visit Sian instead. We were also able to visit three people's communes: the Hsin-chiao People's Commune outside of Canton; the Feng-huo People's Commune some eighty kilometers outside of Sian; and the July First People's Commune outside of Shanghai.

We were the first group of American child psychologists to visit China in a generation. In twenty days, even twenty days as filled with schools, children, and words as ours were, we could see only a corner of the continent of human beings and ideas that is contemporary China. Still, we want to describe our corner of understanding, to present our observations, however partial and incomplete, in as fair and clear a way as we can. We were all moved—some of us shaken—by the differences between Chinese and American societies, differences shown in ideology, in art, in educational practice, and, most vividly of all for us, in the lives of the children. Our notebooks are a jumble of impressions, speculation, and observation; the language of the notes is colorful, even florid, and occasionally intemperate. But we are convinced that our reportorial responsibilities are better served in a report that bends toward the particular and the prosaic rather than the speculative and theoretical. Our understanding of China is limited indeed, our warrant for interpretation slight. Therefore we will stay as close to personal specific observation as we can. Three qualifications to that intention must be added, however. First, each of us did bring back a different theory of Chinese children and we cannot reduce altogether either the variety of views or the tendency to select observations in support of our biases. Second, we cannot, without losing our readers altogether, always indicate the difference between "We saw . . . " and "We were told that . . . ," although we have tried to do so as often as good sense permitted. Finally, all statistical data, demographic, medical, or educational, must be viewed carefully. We did not sample broadly, we were rarely able to confirm the accuracy of the statistics ourselves, and the Chinese do not have a uniform national reporting system. Our numbers, then, are data themselves for conclusions to be drawn in the future.

The structure of the delegation's report is fairly simple. A first section will be given over to some brief notes of historical and conceptual background to our visit. There follow five sections about children in development, specifically in the Chinese family, in nurseries, in kindergartens, in primary schools, and in middle schools. Then two sections focus on matters of special interest—the learning of language in China and some aspects of the delivery of health care to the children. Finally, in the last pages, we present the cast of characters and an itinerary.

We are particularly indebted to our hosts in China, especially to Mr. Hsieh and Mr. Hao, who worked diligently and with notable patience to meet our many requests. Not only did they arrange for us to visit Sian and other unscheduled settings, but time and again they made it possible for us to divide into several small groups according to our particular interests and to meet people with special backgrounds that would enable them to answer our questions. We would also like to express our regrets to the Education Circles of Nanking for not being able to visit them, and to thank once more the hundreds of teachers and children who helped us spin one thread to be woven with others into an emerging portrait of the People's Republic of China.

Back home, we were helped on every side—by Anne Keatley and the Committee on Scholarly Communication, by Ezra Vogel's patient reading and rereading of our drafts, by Julia James' devoted typing, and by the tender care of the Yale University Press. Jane Isay, Cathy Iino, and Sally Sullivan, all of the press, served the people of the delegation with zest, good humor, and skill.

An early form of "productive labor." Preschool children, with impressive dexterity, pack flashlight bulbs made in a nearby factory.

The vegetable garden maintained by students at East-is-Red Kindergarten in Kwangchow.

During primary school years, more hours and more skill go into productive labor; here, a Little Red Soldier paints plastic swans.

The lathe work of middle-school students in part of the school's tool-making factory. The students design as well as construct some of the equipment they use in the factory.

Faculty and students from Sian City Foreign Languages Institute join peasants from Feng-huo People's Commune in the construction of an earth dam. For at least one month a year, college students and their teachers work in factories or on farms.

1. NOTES ON BACKGROUND

We moved here from Yenan. In Yenan we were deeply impressed by the tradition of the Revolution. We lead the children in labor they are able to do. Morally, intellectually, and physically, we teach the children along the directions set by Chairman Mao.

—Director of Sian Kindergarten #1, November 28, 1973

The development of schools and preschool institutions in China must be understood against the background of China's economic goals and problems and the major political events that have occurred since 1949. In the years well before 1949 formal education based on Western models replaced traditional tutoring in the Confucian classics, and many new schools were built. Despite this rapid expansion of "modern" schools, in 1949 much of the male population, particularly in rural areas, and almost all of the female population got little or no schooling, and most Chinese remained illiterate. Those who were in school received a general academic education rather than training in specific work skills to prepare them to tackle China's economic problems. Since women were not encouraged to work, preschool institutions were in this period even more scarce than primary and secondary schools; we were told, for example, that in the entire city of Peking before 1949 there were only fifteen kindergartens and nurseries, with only 2,300 children enrolled.

After their victory in 1949, the Chinese Communists set up an ambitious program of economic development and social transformation. By stages they moved to replace the formerly dominant social classes with new elites drawn from the formerly oppressed and to eliminate private ownership of the means of production. With a huge and densely settled population, at least 80 percent of

1

which was involved directly in agricultural production, and with only a small educated elite, China was faced with the problem of how to make the best use of its available resources to modernize without sacrificing the social goals of an egalitarian socialist society. It was obvious to the new, post-1949 elite that the educational institutions established by the Kuomintang government were not suited to these goals, but agreeing about what kinds of institutions are suitable has not been as easy. Schools and preschool institutions have been near the center of the continuing disputes and conflicts among the leadership over the proper "line" and "road" since 1949, and no consensus has emerged even now.

After 1949 the Chinese Communists implemented a series of reforms in the existing schools. These were taken over militarily and politically, and curricular reforms and thought reform of the teachers and students were carried out. To the existing schools many new ones were added, so that by 1972 ten times as many students as before 1949 were reported to be attending primary school, for a total of 127 million[1]—a figure that means a very high proportion indeed of children of the relevant ages are now in primary school. With the socialization of the economy in 1955–1956 and subsequent labor mobilizations more and more women joined the labor force, necessitating the creation of a large network of preschool child-care institutions; probably the clear majority of Chinese children under the age of seven are, however, still cared for by grandmothers or other relatives or friends, rather than in collective institutions. Our Chinese hosts said they had no national statistics on the number or percentage of children attending nurseries and kindergartens. They said that the rate of attendance was generally higher in the cities than in the rural areas, and in the

---

1. A check of official Chinese enrollment figures for the 1949–50 school year yields a figure of 24,391,000 students in primary schools. (Cited in Leo A. Orleans, *Professional Manpower and Education in Communist China,* Washington: [National Science Foundation, 1961], p. 32.) Since this yields the more modest, though still impressive, increase of enrollment of five times up to 1972, it is unclear what the actual base year Hsiao Ching-jo was using in his "before 1949" calculation during our Peking briefing.

cities we visited the estimates of rate of preschool attendance ranged from 30 to 60 percent. We are far from certain about the inclusiveness and precision of the urban figures we were given and we wondered whether informal group-care arrangements, particularly those in the country, were included in the rough statistics. It seems safe to assume, however, that the majority of preschool-age children are still cared for in a family context. In fact, some observations made by other visitors recently suggest that there may be relatively few nurseries in rural China.

Within the schools there were efforts to develop systematic procedures for moral and political indoctrination and to focus learning more on practical skills than on general education, e.g., by creating a new network of specialized secondary schools turning out technicians, accountants, and so on. But at various times since 1949 the existing schools have been denounced for continuing to place too much stress on academic subjects and not enough on labor and politics, and reforms have catapulted the schools off in new directions. One such major criticism and overhaul took place as part of the ill-fated Great Leap Forward (1958–60) when, under the "Three Red Banners," an attempt was made to bring schooling closer to production.[2]

When these reforms were subsequently watered down or not pursued vigorously enough, the Cultural Revolution (1966–69) arose to advocate changes with a new fervor. Of course, the Cultural Revolution affected far more than education in China, but with the important involvement of the young Red Guards, the closing of the universities and many middle schools, and the transformation of procedures for selecting and training teachers, the Cultural Revolution apparently had profound consequences for Chinese children.

In the years since the Cultural Revolution, schools have been reopened and reformed in an effort to implement the "Maoist

2. The Three Red Banners represented a general policy for the advancement of China—the "great leap" in production, the "general line" for socialist construction, and the formation of people's communes.

line" on education, and at the time of our visit the debates about policy in this area were still going on. In all of the briefings given us, the great divide between pre–Cultural Revolution and post–Cultural Revolution educational policies was given even greater prominence than the earlier great divide, between the pre-1949 and the post-1949 situations, a change uniformly described as "Liberation." To understand what we saw, it is important to consider what the major features of this "Maoist line" in education are, as they were described to us.

Mao Tse-tung's most important statement on education, part of his May 7th (1966) directive, was often cited by our Chinese hosts.

> This holds good for students, too. While their main task is to study, they should in addition to their studies learn other things—that is, industrial work, farming, and military affairs. They should also criticize the bourgeoisie. The period of schooling should be shortened, education should be revolutionized, and the domination of our schools by bourgeois intellectuals should by no means be allowed to continue.[3]

Here we find several of the themes we kept hearing during our visit. Chinese education, led astray by the "revisionist line" of Liu Shao-ch'i (the former president) and Lin Piao (the former minister of defense), was placing too much emphasis on academics. Students spent too long in school, were isolated from their society, and while failing to learn useful skills were developing into arrogant elitists. The solution was to revamp the schools once again so that the students would have what our hosts described as an "all-around" education morally, intellectually, and physically. Graduates of the reformed schools were supposed to have useful work experience and skills and the kind of political zeal and physical tempering needed to fulfill whatever difficult work assignments they might receive from the state. This inculcation of the proper attitudes and traits was expected to begin in preschool in-

---

3. *Peking Review* 32 (August 5, 1966): 7.

stitutions and to carry right on up through the universities. In nurseries and kindergartens, the "revisionist line" consisted in tending mostly to the physical comfort and enjoyment of the children, while neglecting to instill the proper political attitudes and, especially, committment to labor. The remedy proposed was to begin the proper kinds of training as early as possible, in forms, to be sure, suitable to the ages of the children involved. Our hosts frankly admitted that in nurseries—for children under age three—there remains a strong emphasis on physical comfort, and only in the kindergartens—for children three to seven—does education in the Maoist line begin to become important.

The Chinese, like other Marxist believers in the overwhelming influence of the environment in the formation of human beings, have a profound faith in the ability of proper educational procedures to produce desired attitudes, values, and emotions in children. In one summary we were told that a central objective in all schools was to teach students the "Five Loves": of Mao Tsetung, the Chinese Communist Party, the socialist motherland, productive labor, and the workers, peasants, and soldiers. As an afterthought several secondary "loves" and other emotions were added: love of the collective of students, respect for discipline, acceptance of group criticism and dedication to self-criticism, and devotion to internationalism. In the words of the director of Shanghai Middle School #2,

Formerly we put intellectual development first and kept a closed door [a reference to Mao's insistence on an "open door" between the lives of students and the lives of workers, peasants, and soldiers]. The students did not know how the workers worked or how the peasants plowed the fields. Under Chairman Mao's revolutionary lines, we develop the children morally, intellectually, and physically. The students are educated to serve the people wholeheartedly. We also organize the students to take part in the class struggle and the struggle for scientific research; to learn from the workers, peasants, and soldiers; to combine theory with practice.

These attitudes and feelings are expected to be inculcated in countless ways—in lectures, stories, songs, movies, skits, and group discussion and criticism sessions. In many of these forums the specific technique used to create the desired emotional force is called "recalling the bitterness and thinking of the sweetness." This refers to reminding youth of the bitter oppression suffered by many in the pre-1949 society, and then contrasting this with post-1949 progress, not forgetting the danger of class enemies who may bring back the past. The combination of vicarious hatred and gratitude is supposed to provide the emotional force necessary to implant the desired attitudes. Since many teachers are not suitable reporters of the suffering before 1949, as part of the "open door" educational policy in recent years, old workers, peasants, and soldiers are invited to visit the schools and tell their bitter stories.

Another technique is the use of models, and students at all levels are presented with heroes, whom they are encouraged to emulate. During our visit, the most widely publicized hero in schools at all levels was Lei Feng, a soldier who was first presented for emulation in 1964 for his good deeds and constant study of Mao Tse-tung's thought and for his devoted service to his country. Teachers organize students at all levels to discuss the life of Lei Feng and other heroes, comparing their own behavior and that of their classmates with the models. Through such exercises they are expected to develop habits of criticism and self-criticism.

In line with their views on environmental determinism, Chinese Communists reject notions of innate differences in intelligence or potential for learning, and feel that if a child is slow or poorly behaved, it is the fault of bad influences on him, now or in the past. When we spoke our concern about the absence of systematic research on differences among children, in contrast to the substantial investment in agricultural research, one of our hosts remarked that plants were studied because they differed but "it is important for us to believe that all children are the same." Whatever differences result from the impact of early experience can be corrected by mobilizing extra energy and attention to bring the varying student into line with his classmates. Our hosts seemed generally uncomfortable and vague whenever we raised questions about retarded or otherwise exceptional children.

Two other kinds of differences were more openly recognized, differences between the sexes and among children of what had been different social classes before 1949, although here, too, the official line was that a proper education would overcome them. Boys and girls do, we were occasionally and almost reluctantly told, show familiar differences in school behavior; girls are more partial to music and dance and better in verbal subjects, boys are more inclined to rough sports and better in science and mathematics. But ideally teachers are supposed to have the same expectations and demands of students of both sexes. Students from the pre-1949 "bad" classes—landlords, rich peasants, capitalists— are expected to have poorer political attitudes than those from "good classes"—workers and poor and lower middle peasants.[4] But again, the basic educational expectation is that proper pressures can change even the children of the old bourgeoisie into committed members of the present culture.

China wishes to avoid the problem created by the expansion of education in other developing countries, too many graduates turned out by secondary schools and colleges for whom there are no white-collar jobs available and who refuse to accept anything else. In China since the Cultural Revolution the policy has been to encourage youth to complete middle school (upper middle school in the cities, lower middle school in the countryside) but to expect that, upon graduation, they will take up work as manual laborers, often in remote rural areas. Even if the stated goal is reached—

---

4. At the time of land reform (before 1952) the rural population was divided on the basis of their property into formally designated classes: landlord, rich peasant, middle peasant (later divided into upper and lower middle peasant), poor peasant, and agricultural laborer. Since that time the former landlords and rich peasants have been stigmatized as "bad classes," while the former poor and lower middle peasants (and laborers) are favored classes, and former ordinary middle peasants or upper middle peasants are in an intermediate status. A similar classification took place for the urban population.

half the lower-middle school graduates going on to upper middle school—the Chinese will continue to assert the equal merit of work and study. Only after "tempering" themselves in manual labor (or in military service) will a select few middle-school graduates be chosen to go on to the university or to urban jobs. To indicate the scale of this effort to send educated youth from urban to rural areas, we were told that from Shanghai alone over a million secondary school graduates had been sent down to the countryside since 1968. Creating the desired enthusiasm for study combined with the willingness to accept manual labor assignments requires long and concentrated emphasis in the schools. Students at various levels engage in "productive labor," ranging from simple room cleaning and gardening for kindergartners to light manufacturing in workshops and factories in middle schools and universities. Students in middle schools also spend some time each year working in nearby factories or in rural communes. Courses in the curriculum are supposed to be adapted so that they relate directly to work problems: a geometry problem is given based on cutting angles on the school workshop's lathes; a chemistry lesson focuses on plant stimulants. Children are taught songs and stories emphasizing the glories of leaving the towns and cities to serve agriculture and the nobility of the poor and lower middle peasants, in an effort to overcome fears of rural hardships and disdain for peasant backwardness. Some graduates will end up in the army, and most will serve in the militia in their future work units; schools are reported to emphasize military exercises and general physical training. In our visits to Chinese schools, however, we were not shown any specifically military-related activities.

The recent reforms also emphasize the need for local experimentation and adaptation in the curriculum and an open door for local political authorities to supervise school activities. We were told that educational planning has been decentralized since the Cultural Revolution, with fewer specific directives coming from the national government in Peking, where the former ministries of education and higher education have been replaced by the Group on Science and Education under the State Council.[5] Within individual schools the teachers and former administrators share control in an administrative "three way alliance" with members of Workers' Mao Tse-tung Thought Propaganda Teams sent in for extended periods from local factories (and, in the universities, with members of People's Liberation Army Mao Tse-tung Thought Propaganda Teams as well). In addition to insuring that the correct political atmosphere is maintained in the schools in spite of "the bourgeois tendencies of the teachers and administrators," propaganda team members are supposed to play a role in adapting the local curriculum to train students better for their future work roles. At the same time, to combat their bourgeois tendencies, teachers are supposed to engage in regular political study, labor, and group criticism so that they will develop the desired attitudes themselves; they are also expected to go on regular work tours each year to factories or farms. Teachers are also supposed to change their relationship with students, becoming comradely advisors who stimulate the students to derive the most from their school experience, rather than autocratic figures who use unannounced examinations to test how well lessons have been memorized. The former isolation of schools from society is supposed to be broken down as well, both by shortening the period of study and by drawing students from the immediate local neighborhoods, in contrast to the policy before the Cultural Revolution, when certain "key schools" drew their students from wide areas by competitive examination.

All of these changes obviously necessitate new priorities in the system of selection and promotion of students. Although grades and examinations still exist, relatively less stress is said to be placed on the sheer absorption of academic knowledge, and more stress on whether students have the proper political attitudes and enthusiasm. From an early age, teachers' evaluations and selection

---

5. During the National People's Congress (January, 1975), the Ministry of Education was re-established.

for student offices, and from lower-middle-school graduation on, selection for further schooling, all are supposed to depend to a large extent on student zeal in labor and political activities. The goal is to produce "revolutionary successors," youths who, in very different circumstances of the culture, will continue to bear the kinds of attitudes and motivations borne by the guerrilla fighters of the period before 1949. To produce such revolutionary successors is said to take constant effort and attention, in preschool institutions as well as schools, and in extracurricular activities as well as in in-school activities.

A note on the administration of Chinese education

There seemed to be some consensus that the basic model for the administration of a school after the Cultural Revolution has been the "three-in-one" Revolutionary Committee. Members of the School Committee are drawn from the following groups: workers, elected from nearby factories; cadres (e.g., the former principals), the people who alone make up school administration before the Cultural Revolution; and "the masses"—teachers, students, and staff workers in the school. In one case (Peking Middle School #31) we were told that the Revolutionary Committee contained one factory worker, six cadres, three teachers, five students, and a staff worker. In justification of the arrangement, we were told (by Chang Yu-ju, November 22, 1973) that

> the cadres have certain experiences in administration and the workers have the line of the proletariat. The good points of the cadres can be kept and the bad points criticized. The masses can bring in the ideas of the students and teachers and carry the decisions to the masses. One man's wisdom does not equal that of the masses.

A similar pattern was found throughout our visit, though it was not clear whether workers typically sat on the Revolutionary Committees of kindergartens. Two other patterns seemed relatively stable. Whatever variation existed in makeup of the School Revolutionary Committees, the three functions of the group were invariably politics (ideology), curriculum (education), and general administration. And there was always an executive (or standing) committee of the Revolutionary Committee, which met often (perhaps once or twice a week) to oversee the operation of the school.

Our observations clearly do not warrant general conclusions about school administration in China, but they suggest that within a strong structural uniformity ("three-in-one" administration) some local variation exists. Further, and here our evidence is even weaker, there seems to be a single person in day-to-day charge, more often than not the member of the committee with responsibility for ideological matters.

The delegation had almost no direct contact with the national administration for education and it was difficult for us to assess either the degree or method of central direction of local schools. We were told emphatically that the system was "decentralized" and that the apparently very small staff in Peking had nothing to do with running schools or universities. However, some control through the purse was suggested by the testimony that the Peking group was charged with "planning, reform, policy, and budget." An official confirmed the general accuracy of the representation of administrative structure on page 12.[6] From Provincial Bureau (at least) on down to the particular school, the basic administrative division was, as noted earlier, into sections on politics, curriculum, and general administration.

---

6. See footnote 5.

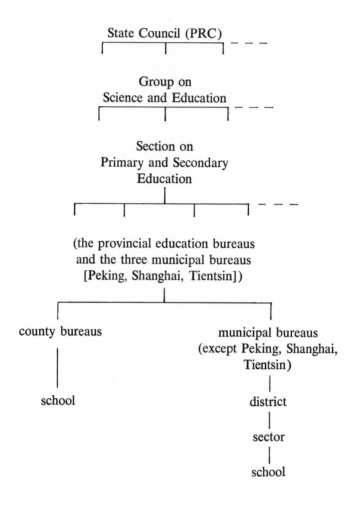

State Council (PRC)

Group on
Science and Education

Section on
Primary and Secondary
Education

(the provincial education bureaus
and the three municipal bureaus
[Peking, Shanghai, Tientsin])

county bureaus

municipal bureaus
(except Peking, Shanghai,
Tientsin)

school

district

sector

school

The American delegation was a spectacle for curious and enthusiastic Chinese. The little children were at once watchful and calm.

Mothers and children at a dairy commune; the row of their homes is in the background.

The livingroom–bedroom of a worker's family in an urban factory complex. Though the decorations are more varied than those we typically saw, the room contains elements common to all the homes we visited—the picture of Mao Tse-tung, family photographs, a few books on politics, and the thermos essential for making tea.

2. THE CHINESE FAMILY

There was a foolish old man who lived at the foot of a mountain that blotted out the sun. One day the villagers saw the old man digging away at the mountain.

"Oh, you foolish old man!" they said. "You cannot dig the mountain away."

But the old man replied, "The mountain, it will not get bigger, And if my children and you, my neighbors, help me dig, then in time it will no longer hide the sun."

—One version of a folk story told to Chinese children and the basis of an oft quoted article by Mao Tse-tung.

Our report on Chinese families moves from a general summary through particular observation to tentative interpretation. Throughout, we are highly sensitive about the fragility of our sampling procedures (if they can properly be so called) and of our observational base. The margins should carry continuously the message, "Within the constraints of our opportunities, we believe . . . "

Sources of our information and their limitations

Our opportunities to collect information about family life in China were limited. On visits to the Feng-huo Brigade outside Sian and to the July First People's Commune in suburban Shanghai we split into five groups for lunch in peasant households, with an hour or two for conversation during and after the meal. On visits to two new workers' villages in Shanghai we spent several hours interviewing families in their homes. We made briefer visits to families in other settings, and during some of our visits to schools parents were present to answer occasional questions.

15

We always asked teachers about relations between the family and the school, patterns of family versus collective preschool child care, and the family's role in the extracurricular lives of children. In formal briefings by neighborhood educational officials we tried to get numerical data on incidence and patterns of home and group care. And, of course, we talked informally to many of the interpreters and local officials who accompanied us about their families and their views on child rearing.

All told, we observed or interviewed about twenty families and these came predominantly from two communes and two workers' settlements. We usually went to apartments to which we were directed rather than, say, picking households at random, although on two occasions we made spur-of-the-moment visits that could not have been easily anticipated. We are not certain to what extent the families we visited were representative even of their immediate neighborhoods, but the sometimes unexpected nature of our requests and the uncertainty of our local guides about whom we would find at home give us some confidence that the families interviewed were not grossly atypical of their areas.

Obviously the appearance at the door of foreigners with a retinue of interpreters and officials is an unnatural situation in any society. In our visits to families we were not able, as we were in some kindergartens and schools, simply to sit back for long periods of time and observe the round of daily activities. And because in contacts with outsiders like us the Chinese tend to use a fair amount of the common ideological language, penetrating the underlying social reality was difficult and some kinds of questions we could not even hope to ask (for example, "How often do you spank your children?" or "Do some parents in this area still play the major role in picking spouses for their children?"). Given these problems in observation and interpretation, we justify reporting our impressions on two grounds: first, even our patchwork of findings may be of use in reducing our present ignorance about Chinese families, and second, the family is of such obvious importance for child care, in China as elsewhere, that we would leave too great a gap if we did not speak of families.

The family in city and country

There are no comprehensive demographic statistics available to help us describe family structure in China. Perhaps the most significant variations we were able to observe (we did not visit national minority areas) were those between city and countryside.

It seems easier to generalize about rural family structure than about urban. Rural families in China live in hamlets and villages upon which the three-tiered structure of commune, production brigade, and production team has often been superimposed. In most cases, the primary unit for purposes of accounting and organizing work activities is the lowest level, the team, a unit of perhaps 20 to 40 households corresponding to a small village or to a neighborhood within a larger village. The Feng-huo Brigade outside Sian was an atypical case, in which the brigade—270 households and 1,225 people—and not the team was the basic accounting unit. In the Feng-huo Brigade we also saw some new apartments being built to rehouse the population, whereas in most communes the peasants continue to live in individual homes. The houses tend to be clustered together, with the public fields surrounding the settlements and perhaps with some small private agricultural plots nearby.

The dwellings we saw in the countryside were of varied construction, using combinations of sun-dried mud bricks, bricks, wood, and tile. Outside Sian we saw a few homes built into the clay hillsides, a traditional form of housing in the area. Floors may be concrete, packed earth, wood, or a combination of materials. In the communes we visited, the most common house layout was for the front door to open into a combined sitting and dining room; a kitchen was behind this room and bedrooms opened off on one or both sides of it. We did not see many of the traditional household compounds ringing a central courtyard. The sitting and dining room contained few furnishings besides a table and low stools (and, in the case of a few families, a coffin). This area was also used for storage of tools, grain, and so on. In the homes we visited, cooking was done over brick or concrete ovens with materials such as cornstalks and straw the most common fuel. In the Feng-huo Brigade, these ovens were also used to heat the traditional k'ang sleeping platforms. The families we visited generally had bedrooms separate from the common room, but with the children sometimes sharing a room with an aged relative or with the parents. The bedroom furnishings were simple—for example, pictures (of Mao Tse-tung and family members), thermos bottles, blankets, mosquito netting. We also saw a fair number of bicycles, occasionally a treadle sewing machine. The homes we saw all had electric lighting, although electricity is not always available year round or at all hours and the rooms are dimly lit when all the lights are on.

There are a number of basic variations of family structure in the countryside. We were told in the communes we visited that it was still the general practice for brides to move to their husbands' village to live, though the decision might be affected by availability of housing. Whether one or more married sons live in the house of their parents or set up separate households nearby seems to be more variable. The three communes were reported to have, on the average, from four to six people in each household. Aged parents seem generally to live with one of their married children, receiving economic support while helping with child care and domestic tasks. There are minimal welfare provisions for aged peasants who have no relatives to care for them; there is no uniform retirement or pension policy in the countryside, and the aged continue to do some work in the public fields as long as they are able, earning work points in proportion to their efforts. At the Feng-huo Brigade we were shown an "old-folks work group" of six men in their seventies tending the brigade orchards. Old peasants who are unable to work on the public fields do not, of course, earn this income, and depend on the support of younger relatives, as in ages past, or if they are without relatives, on commune welfare.

The general rural pattern is one of stable two, three, and four generation families. Divorces, we were told, are very few, but some family members are drawn off for military service or for work in nearby towns and cities. Membership of rural families is sometimes increased when children of preschool age are sent by their urban parents to be cared for by rural relatives. Most peasants, it seems, after finishing school can count on going directly to work in the commune's fields, or in the offices, schools, or enterprises run by the commune (for example, tool, cement, and brick factories, poultry hatcheries, carpentry shops). Employees in these nonagricultural operations earn wages that are more stable than the peasants' work points, the value of which fluctuates with the harvests, but apparently not much higher than those of skilled field hands. Some positions, such as a brigade cadre or a barefoot doctor, are part-time and are joined with labor in the fields. It seems that almost all able-bodied women, as well as men, work in the fields during peak agricultural seasons. Thus the average rural family may have two or more active laborers plus young children and sometimes an aged parent or two, with the adults and older children sharing in domestic tasks and work on private plots.

We were told several times that the recommended minimum ages of marriage for rural youths are twenty-three for females and twenty-five for males. Couples are asked to have only two children, and to space those at fairly wide intervals, but our guides said that compliance had been slow and incomplete, a judgment confirmed universally by other visitors. As is so often the case, officials were apt, optimistically enough, to state goals rather than achievements. As with retirement, rural regulations on maternity leave vary. In one commune 56 days rest after birth was provided, as in state industries, while in another 100 days was recommended, because of the physical strain of agricultural labor. In neither case were any works points or wages paid to women during the period of maternity leave.

In rural villages primary schools are apparently common; there is sometimes a lower middle school, and, probably even more rarely, a nursery and kindergarten. There were kindergartens everywhere we visited (remember, we were the "kindergarten delegation"), but the reports of our hosts and the observations of other visitors suggest that a relatively small proportion of rural children under seven are in formal group care. Who, then, cares for the millions of preschool children who are not in formal group care in a country where almost all women are said to be in productive labor? We do not know and can only speculate that the traditional care-givers still give care—grandmothers, siblings, neighbors, and mothers who work only part-time. In any case, the size and quality of the rural preschool institutions seems to be quite variable, depending to a considerable extent upon the prosperity of the commune and its subordinate brigades and teams.

In urban areas, residential patterns and family forms are more varied than they seemed to be in the countryside. We visited three types of urban dwellings. We saw old-style housing in a Peking residential neighborhood, where a gate opened onto a courtyard bordered by rows of tile-roofed houses. Some families had lived in their compounds since before 1949; other compounds formerly belonging to single well-to-do families had been split up after 1949 to house several families. A second type of housing we saw was the factory dormitory or apartment compound—housing provided for employees and their dependents near the factory. We were told that this is a fairly common pattern for bureaucratic offices as well as factories. A third pattern is represented by the workers' villages we visited in Shanghai; these apartment compounds were built and administered by the city and space was assigned through work units.

The social homogeneity of neighbors appeared to be highest in the factory apartment houses, while neighborhood self-sufficiency (in terms of shops, service enterprises, and parks, for example) seemed to be greatest in the new workers' villages. In all settings living space is often quite cramped, with the sitting room doubling as a bedroom and the beds taking up much of the space. By any calculation, some beds were used by more than two people. Bathrooms and kitchens may be shared with adjacent households; in older style houses, going to the toilet may require a trip to a public facility on the street. Heating varies, with radiators common in the newer apartments, but traditional coal-ball stoves the rule in older housing. Similarly, cooking fuel varies from gas in newer residences to coal ball in older. Furnishings were only slightly more abundant than in the rural homes we visited; there were extra blankets, pictures, mirrors, thermos bottles, bicycles, sometimes a radio or a sewing machine, usually a few political books or pamphlets and, in families with children, a few toys. The impression is generally one of perfectly clean, somewhat spartan comfort.

Perhaps the most frequent family composition we encountered was the nuclear family with a grandmother or another relative—for example, an unmarried sibling of the husband or wife. Also common was the complete three-generation family of older parents, son or daughter, spouse, and children. We saw a number of variants on the pattern; in one case, a couple and their children lived with the widowed mothers of both the husband and wife. Some old couples lived alone, a practice made possible by the existence of retirement benefits not available in rural areas, and we saw a number of instances of old retired couples caring for a grandchild or two, or living with a married child (or child-in-law), while the other spouse was stationed elsewhere because of military service, job requirements, or political reeducation. We encountered a variety of such cases of husband–wife separation, either for long or short periods. Such arrangements may contribute both to the flexibility of urban families and the continuing importance of extended kin ties in the urban setting. Our impression of fairly frequent husband–wife separations was balanced by our impression of stability of residence. Urban families seem to grow and shrink in response to personnel transfers as well as to births and deaths, but at least some members of the family will often have lived in the same residence for fifteen or more years. It was difficult for us mobile Americans to comprehend that even in the hearts of big cities, people lived in functional neighborhoods, tied together by long acquaintance, shared service, and similar histories. The continued existence of stable neighborhoods may be an important reason why social groups exert so powerful an influence in China.

In the cities, the recommended minimum ages for marriage are about twenty-five for females and twenty-eight for males, and, as in the rural areas, two children, fairly widely spaced, is the official ideal. In our visits we found these norms fairly well adhered to, but we cannot be certain of the selectivity of our information. For what it is worth, observations on the streets of four cities over three weeks yielded only two confirmed sightings of pregnant women, although loose clothing makes detection more difficult than in most cultures. Our guides implied that the birth-control campaign was being more uniformly, vigorously, and successfully pushed in the cities than in the countryside. Cramped living quarters, marital separations, and tight wages may contribute to limited family size as well; even the families we saw with school-age children (i.e., children born before the recent birth-control campaign) tended to fit the ideal of two children.

Most physically able urban adults are employed; we were told at various points that over 90 percent of the women under forty-five were employed. Women who did not work in earlier years are now often employed in small factories run by the neighborhood (for example, sewing factories or small tool factories), and we got the definite impression that wages and benefits in these factories are lower than in state-financed factories. In the factory housing we visited, either husband or wife might work in the factory, and if one partner did not, he (or more often, she) might work in a related, subsidiary street factory. Husbands and wives who lived in the workers' villages also were often reported to work in different units. Women employed in state factories are entitled to a fifty-six-day maternity leave with pay, and some work units have feeding rooms or nurseries to permit resumption of work while a baby is still being nursed. Whether young children are sent to nurseries and kindergartens depends on a variety of factors—availability of facilities (some preschool institutions have to select from a large number of applicants), family finances (in the places we visited, fees for tuition, food, and materials ranged from about eight to sixteen yuan per month—that is, about 15 percent of a two-worker income), and the availability of parents or alternative caretakers. The estimates we got of preschool attendance levels were often vague, but as we noted earlier, were generally well under 50 percent. In most cases, nurseries, kindergartens, and schools serve the children in the immediate neighborhood, although some of the more highly regarded kindergartens seemed to have a disproportional number of children from official families. There are still boarding nurseries and kindergartens, but boarding primary and middle schools have been largely discontinued in urban areas, and children apparently go home for lunch.

Urban men may retire at sixty and women between fifty and fifty-five (at the younger age for manual-labor jobs). Employees in state enterprises receive pensions of 70 percent of their final wages if they have enough seniority, reduced percentages for shorter services. Workers at retirement age may request to stay at their jobs, or they may be assigned to such activities as instructing pupils in school labor courses. Even those returning to their families are supposed to be organized for regular neighborhood political study and to supervise the after-school activities of local youths. The impression we gained was that, unless health problems intervened, retired people did not retreat from society into their homes to rest.

Some family vignettes

Perhaps the delicate balance between our limited evidence and our emerging sense of regularities can best be sustained by narrating, in brief summary, several of our visits. Later we will draw out some propositions about Chinese families that are congruent with the accounts given here and our other observations.

VIGNETTE 1: A DAY IN THE LIFE OF A THREE-GENERATION FAMILY. We were in a worker's village in Shanghai; it was midmorning on a weekday, and our two local hosts ran ahead to inquire where there might be a family with young children and mother at home. There were two circumstances in our favor; a substantial number of workers in China have their regular days off on weekdays instead of on Sunday, and many others work on late or night shifts, thus they might be at home and available at this morning hour. Our escort returned with good news; she had found a family with young children in which not only the mother, but also the father was home.

We were welcomed warmly into a bedroom–living room now filled to capacity, for in addition to the visitors there were four smiling adults, all greeting us at once, and two children, a three-year-old boy and a six-month-old girl. The father and mother appeared to be in their early thirties. Both parents were at home because neither worked on a morning shift: the wife was employed in a medicine factory from two forty-five in the afternoon till ten-thirty at night; the husband worked on the night shift at a dyeing plant. Although he was up and around in the late morning and early afternoon, it quickly became apparent that major responsibility for the care of the older child was taken by the maternal grandmother, a genial woman who beamed on the entire gathering and exchanged side-talk with an age-mate who turned out to be the next-door neighbor, also a grandmother.

What happened yesterday? We asked the parents to give us a picture of one day's life in their family; they told us about the previous day.

Grandmother got up at six, went to market for milk, and returned about an hour later to help the three-year-old get dressed and to prepare breakfast. At about the same time, the father returned from his night shift. At eight, the mother woke, dressed and fed the baby, and put her back in bed for three hours. The family had breakfast (the boy ate porridge with milk), and afterward grandmother took her grandson for a walk in the park. By nine, the father had gone to bed, mother was busy with housework and knitting, and when grandmother and grandson returned from their walk, the grandmother washed the dishes and began to prepare the midday meal. While the adults were busy, the grandson looked at children's books, then went out to play with other children on the block. At eleven-thirty the baby awoke and was tended by mother. At noon, the family, except for sleeping father, ate their midday meal.

In the early afternoon the grandson took a nap and mother

left by bus for her factory, taking the baby with her. When the boy woke up at three, grandmother gave him a snack, after which he went out in the neighborhood to play for about an hour. When he returned, grandmother, who is illiterate, told him stories from a picture book. At four-thirty father woke up, washed the boy's quilt, and played with his son for awhile.

We interrupted to ask what else the father did in the home, and were told that he often helped with the cooking, washed diapers, and sewed the children's clothes. Indeed, he had made the attractive shirt and pants that his son was wearing. As these were displayed we could see the six layers the child wore for warmth.

Relation between adults and children within the family. Throughout the interview, there was much attention given to the two children by all three adult members of the family. During the visit, the baby remained in her mother's arms; she did not cry once for the entire hour and a half we were together (including the subsequent visits to other apartments, and the picture taking outdoors). The mother's manner was assured and affectionate. Occasionally, she would look at the baby, cuddle her closer, or amuse her with a soft rubber animal toy. The three-year-old boy alternated between periods of activity with toys and furniture and periods of being held, first by the grandmother, and then by the father. In his play, the boy improvised with an empty chair he carried about, placing it sideways on the floor as a kind of stable for the toy horse he pulled about on a string. All three adults spoke to the boy frequently and were very affectionate with him; the father, at one point, took him upon his knee and gave him the baby's pink-faced rubber animal.

By contrast, no one except the mother paid much attention to the baby, and even she seemed to be more concerned with keeping the baby comfortable than with engaging her attention, a pattern we often observed in the treatment of infants in China and consistent with the view we heard expressed on several occasions by nursery-school personnel that in the first year of life "children can't do very much."

Next-door neighbors. We never heard what the family had done on the evening of the previous day because of the arrival of more next-door neighbors. It turned out that there were three families living on the second floor—two retired couples, each in a single room, and the family we were visiting, which occupied two rooms. All shared the use of a centrally located communal kitchen and toilet. The three families were clearly on intimate terms, and there was so much joking and laughter that our interpreter smilingly threw up her hands. We could not leave without visiting everyone's apartment in turn. When we asked to take a picture, they came together as a group, placing the young parents and the two children in the middle. They stayed together as they said good-bye with waves and good wishes.

We were told later that the retired workers in this and other housing projects took special responsibility for the children of the neighborhood. We were told, for example, that as the children walked to and from kindergarten and school, the oldsters would greet them on their way, look after the smallest ones, and strike up conversations with older ones to ask about their work at school and to talk about their own experience in the "time of bitterness."

VIGNETTE 2: A DAY IN ANOTHER THREE-GENERATION FAMILY.   An interview with another family in the same housing project shed more light on household economics, the role of the grandfather, and problems of discipline. There are five people in the family, the grandfather and grandmother, sixty-two and sixty-one years old respectively, their daughter, the daughter's husband, and the granddaughter, age two.

A typical day. The grandfather is the first to rise, usually getting up between five and five-thirty in the morning. His granddaughter frequently gets up with him. After exercises, he goes to the vegetable market to shop (our interpreter explained that in China one shops every day) and then the grandmother cooks breakfast. At eight, just before the daughter and her husband go to work, the grandparents do the household chores. The granddaughter helps to clean the floor with a little broom, and when laundry is being done, a handkerchief is put in a basin for her to wash.

After the chores, on Monday, Wednesday, and Friday, there is newspaper reading in the courtyard by literate workers. This was organized by ten or twenty retired workers and is an occasion both for spreading information and for improving the literacy of those who have some degree of ability to read. One afternoon per week there is political study, in which, we were told, one learns "to serve the people."

After lunch the grandparents and the granddaughter take a two hour nap. Neither parent comes home for lunch since there is a dining room at work. Lunch is generally prepared by the grandmother. In the afternoon the grandfather frequently takes the little girl to the park; grandmother sews.

On Sundays, the grandfather goes fishing if the weather is good, sometimes taking his granddaughter along. Apparently he goes with other retired workers. On other occasions, the whole family may go to the movies, to see a dance performance (put on by a propaganda team) or "downtown to shop." On these occasions all five members go together. Occasionally they also go to the zoo.

When students come home from school, the grandfather told us, he helps organize their activities in the neighborhood and "teaches bitterness" to them, that is, he describes how hard life was before 1949, in order to make the younger generation appreciate and sustain the Revolution.

The parents come home at five or soon thereafter, except for the two days a week they are involved in political meetings after work. In general, the grandparents cook in the evening. They apparently take turns in the kitchen as with other household tasks. After supper, the little girl may play with her father or mother but generally goes to bed by eight o'clock. We were told that she likes to have her grandmother put her to bed.

Child care and discipline. We asked whether the grandparents ever spank the child. They replied that they never spank because Chairman Mao says that one should persuade children. The husband said, "In the old society parents beat their children and husbands and wives even beat each other," but that is no longer satisfactory. "If one beats a child it may make the child obedient but it does no good." We asked how one could reason with so young a child and the grandfather acknowledged that it was more a matter of persuading the child to do what it ought to do. He noted that if the granddaughter has a temper tantrum they just let her cry; they can persuade her when she is exhausted. We asked whether they ever give the child candy to persuade her to do what they want. We noted that she was eating candy on several occasions while we were talking with the grandparents. They acknowledged that they do let her eat candy but said they do not bribe her with it. They felt that this would be a very bad thing to do.

We inquired who is most strict in dealing with the child and the grandfather immediately said that he is. He stressed the need for her to learn to do productive labor very early. When we asked about possible disputes between the grandparents and the parents, the grandfather did think the parents sometimes gave the grand-daughter too many different things to eat, but then said that in general they follow his instructions. Clearly he regards himself as the authority in the family, despite his illiteracy and the relatively high educational status of his children.

Since both the grandmother and the grandfather seem to have a busy and, from their account, a very enjoyable round of daily and weekly activities, we asked them how they felt about retirement and whether it was more fun to be retired or to be working. The grandfather's reply was that he enjoyed both lives. In the old days, he noted, working was hard and workers were not respected. But now workers are respected. Likewise, in the old days there was no possibility of retirement, but now they are able to live very comfortably.

VIGNETTE 3: FOUR GENERATIONS IN A COMMUNE. We were at the July First People's Commune; we had just visited many of their agricultural and manufacturing enterprises and were about to be divided into groups of two Americans and an inter-preter to visit various families for the noonday meal. On the way we passed the nursery, in front of which was a group of young mothers, each holding her baby in her arms. They had just come in from the fields for the noonday break, had nursed their infants, and were now walking with them in the warming sun. Farther on were other young women sitting and crocheting, the upper, sharp end of each needle covered with a styrofoam ball that danced in the sun as the needle moved back and forth. Some had two- or three-year-olds close at hand. In front of one of the single-story stucco bungalows sat an ancient peasant woman, a white kerchief round her wrinkled, smiling face. She was winding yarn from a swift. As the wheel became empty, one or another young child would appear, bringing a new skein and removing the finished product. It was a scene of happy industry, but we wondered who was cooking dinner.

We discovered immediately, for the small bungalow was the one in which we were to have our meal. The family consisted of a husband and wife in their early thirties, who had just come home from work—he at the farm tool factory, she at the dairy farm—their two-and-a-half-year-old daughter, the husband's younger sister, who looked in her late twenties, a grandmother, age sixty-two, was busy in the kitchen preparing dinner over a clay stove fueled with straw blown by a bellows, and the old lady out front, who was the great-grandmother and over ninety. The bungalow had four rooms around three sides of a central courtyard open to the outside. There was the usual bedroom–living room, in which we were served tea, and in which the young couple and their baby slept, another room for the grandparents (the grandfather, who is sixty-three, still works in town and would not be home until evening), a kitchen, and one large bedroom, newly but sparsely furnished, which the husband's younger sister seemed to have all to herself. Our translator whispered to us later in a half-happy, half-embarrassed voice that the younger sister was shortly to be married and the room had been prepared for her and her husband.

One day in the life of a commune family. As we sipped our tea, the young mother described a typical day. She got up at five forty-five and washed and dressed her little girl, ate breakfast (usually prepared by the grandparents) and was off to work by seven-fifteen. The father had already left by seven, but had managed to wash the baby's clothes before departing for work. At seven-thirty, the grandmother took the little girl to the nursery a few blocks away. Sometimes the child walks the whole distance, sometimes she has to be carried part way. The grandmother also picks up the child from the nursery before eleven, when the mother gets back for lunch. The husband joins them by eleven-thirty. The grandmother usually prepares the midday meal during the morning.

We asked whether she had had any help that day, when there were so many additional people. Yes, she said, an older daughter had had the day off, and had come early, in time to make the family's breakfast. After the midday meal, the parents return to work, and around twelve-thirty, the grandmother again takes the child to the nursery. Yesterday the little one was picked up by her father at four, but usually one of the two grandparents brings her home.

The evening meal, at which the whole family is present, is usually cooked by the grandparents. While they cook, the little girl plays with older children outdoors. Just before five o'clock, the mother comes home from the dairy, washes the baby, and they all sit down to the main meal of the day.

The day before, after dinner, they had gone to see a film. They usually take their child, but this time she had stayed home with the grandparents. So that the girl would not be disappointed, the parents had had to sneak away. We asked what the film was about. "About bandits who wanted to dynamite a train. They were out-witted by the People's Liberation Army."

We asked what the parents usually did in the evenings. The mother normally knits and the father reads the newspapers, but, of course, on three nights a week there are political studies from five until seven. At the last meeting there had been a summing up of production for the previous month and an allocation of work points. The total profit of the cooperative fluctuates as a function of seasonal production, but last year, at this particular commune, the average income for each household was about 440 dollars.

Child care and discipline. We asked who usually put the child to bed. It was the grandmother, who told her stories. Last night this didn't work; the little girl wanted to stay up to wait for her parents. We inquired whether she objected to the parents' leaving at other times. The mother replied that her little daughter frequently became irritated when it was time for the mother to go to work. She didn't want the mother to leave and insisted on being held.

In response to a question about where the child slept, we were told that she was still in the parents' room, but once she became six years old, she would sleep with the grandmother. "That's the custom in the countryside." Upon inquiry, we learned that the custom applied to boys as well.

We asked about discipline and whether or not there were any differences among the adults in the family on this score. The mother said that the parents sometimes spanked the child, and that the grandparents objected to this. In fact, her husband spanked the child more often than she, and she had complained to him about being too strict.

We asked what sort of behavior the child had been punished for, but, perhaps because the translator misunderstood, we got an answer to a somewhat different question: "Parents should be concerned about the needs of the children. For example, they should let a child go with them to the cinema only if the child has taken a nap." The mother added that she often pointed out other children in the neighborhood as models for her daughter to emulate.

The questions turned to the daughter's development. She had walked at fifteen months and said her first word at about the same time. The mother was now teaching her to read. Toilet training had been completed at a year and a half. As if to demonstrate the point, the little girl, who had been sucking on a candy and playing with toys during the long interview, wandered over to the other side of the room and, in plain view, plunked herself down on a potty.

The mother told us that the little girl now helps in cleaning up (for example, carrying the dustpan). And, with a smile in the child's direction, the mother added, "She likes to sing and dance and dress herself prettily."

We asked about the husband's role in the care of the child (he had not participated in our conversations during tea, but joined us later at the dinner table). The mother replied that "in this situation both mother and father should be equal and help each other." We were not able to follow up the answer since we were at that point invited into the courtyard to have dinner, a sumptuous meal of half a dozen courses. Throughout, as during the tea that had preceded, the doors and windows were lined with curious on-lookers, mostly school-age children but also some adults and old people. They seemed less interested in our conversations, which would have been difficult to hear, than in simply having a look at the strange appearance and attire of the visitors.

Over dinner, the conversation turned to relations between family and school. The mother reported that the teacher visited the home quite often to tell her how her daughter was behaving and "what kinds of toys she likes." The mother then added, in a slightly disapproving tone, that sometimes her daughter asked for another toy every three or four days. She would tell the daughter that grandma had had seven children who often had no clothes to wear. Teachers also held after-school meetings for the parents, at which they would "rerun lessons and play" carried out in the nursery and coach the parents in conducting the same kinds of activities in the home.

As we prepared to leave, we asked the mother what she hoped her child would be when she grew up. She replied that future work would be arranged by the Party, and her daughter "will do whatever work is needed."

VIGNETTE 4. THE MOTHER'S RETURN. We visited a family in a second workers' housing project in Shanghai. The only child in the family was an attractive four-year-old boy, who impressed us by his obvious high intelligence, curiosity, and language skill.

We asked the mother how she happened to be at home, and she replied that she was on a month's vacation (apparently the annual reuniting of work-separated spouses, although a month's time off is said to be unusually long). The factory in which the young mother was working had been moved to a city in another province (Anhwei). Since there were no vacancies in the kindergarten, the young mother had been compelled to leave her four year old in Shanghai. "During the daytime, his grandmother looks after him; at night, his father." The young mother had seen neither her child nor her husband for six months.

We asked whether she and her own mother had any disagreements about how the child should be raised. The mother replied that there were some differences between the generations. She thought the grandparents tended to spoil the child. For example, when she wanted the child to read or listen to children's programs on the radio and the child preferred to play outside, the grandmother would say, "Let him go out." Asked for a second example, the mother stated that sometimes her son irritated her and she spanked him. Then the mother-in-law became angry and would intervene, saying, "You have only one son. It's no good to beat the child. Let him go out."

A request for an account of yesterday's events brought out that, since the grandmother was illiterate, she had asked the husband's brother to read to the child. The children's program on the radio that day had been a story about educated youth going to the countryside. An old man who "belonged to the old society" tried to dissuade them. "It's interesting," the mother commented, "he (the little boy) could sense that he was a 'baddy.'" As in other families, the father was described as helping with household chores, in this case doing dishes and mending clothes. He also cut his son's hair.

The mother's account of the end of the day provided an important reminder. After the little boy was in bed, she taught him a new song, "about a little boy at midnight who was happy and laughing in his dream. When his mother asked him what had made him so happy he told her he had been dreaming of Chairman Mao." We asked whether she had sung any other songs and what they were about. "Yes, I sang to him about the Little Red Soldiers

doing morning exercises, about defending the country, and building the socialist revolution."

VIGNETTE 5: PARENTHOOD VERSUS PEASANTHOOD. At a
rural production brigade eighty kilometers from Sian, we had seen
the carefully tended fields of cotton and corn, the well-fed pigs
in their well-fenced stockades, and the orchard of fruit trees cared
for by old men. Now we were being driven along a dry river bed,
flanked by steep banks and hills seemingly incapable of supporting any growth, but carefully scalloped and terraced in preparation for planting and reclamation. We were on our way to a dam
the brigade was building in order to reclaim still more land for
agricultural use. Scattered across the wide river bed and up the
banks on either side were hundreds of people of all ages busy
shoveling, grading, and pushing heavy wheel barrows. There was
only one piece of machinery not powered by human hands, an
excavator far up the cliffside. All of the earth moving and construction was being done by hand. The period allotted for the entire enterprise was fifty days, but we were told it would be
completed well ahead of time.

Our interpreter had told us that some of the students at the Sian
Foreign Language Institute, where he was an English teacher,
had been sent to this commune for one month to do their annual
agricultural labor. In two groups, they alternated study and labor
day by day.

Suddenly, at a wave from our translator, large numbers of
young people separated themselves from the laboring mass and ran
toward us. There were 150 of them, we were told later. A small
group gathered about each of us and began to converse in quite
good English. We were surprised, for in response to our question,
they replied that they had been studying at the university level for
only one year. We learned that the students were all in their early
twenties. We asked one of them, a young man in a PLA uniform,
what was he doing at the commune. He said, "I am doing productive labor and learning from the peasants." It sounded like a
pat answer, so we decided to push a little. "Can you give us an
example of what you have learned from the peasants?"

"Oh, yes," came the reply, "I can give you two examples. You know the peasants have shared their homes with us. They are very kind. In the family with whom I live the little girl, who is two years old, became sick. The father asked the mother to stay home from the fields to care for the daughter. But the mother answered, 'The little girl is ours, but the fields belong to the people. I shall go to the fields.' That is what I learned from the peasants."

"And what is your second example?"

"Before, I lived with another family, and while I was working in the fields I got sick. The mother in that family walked fifteen kilometers to the village to buy me some pork, which she brought home and cooked for me because I was working as a peasant."

Later we ran into our friends again as they were having a group English lesson in the courtyard after lunch. As in the schools we visited, the text was all on revolutionary themes. Afterward the students chased after us with a request that we sing them a song in English. We sang "Deep Blue Sea," and asked them to sing a Chinese song for us. After a brief consultation, they responded gaily, "Yes, we shall sing you a Chinese song in English." The first stanza ran

On Peking's golden hill
        Shines light forth far and wide
Chairman Mao is the bright golden sun
        Oh how warm, oh how kind
Lighting up our peasants' hearts
        We are marching on the broad and happy socialist road
        Baza hei!

They sang with joy and conviction.

Role allocations

The role of the grandparent. In most of the families we interviewed in which there were young children, the grandmother carried some responsibility for the care of the preschool child once it had been weaned. Of course, ours was a biased sample: we had asked our hosts to look for families in which there were young children at home, and in China, if both parents work fulltime, youngsters of preschool age are not likely to be in their own homes during the day unless a grandparent, or some other relative, is available to care for the child. In the absence of systematic data either at the national or local level, we took advantage of the opportunity at a conference with a group of five kindergarten teachers to ask how many of the children in their classes were brought up primarily by their grandmothers. Four of the teachers estimated between one-quarter and one-third, the remaining one said between fifteen and twenty percent.

There seems little doubt that the grandparent plays a significant role in child rearing, especially for youngsters of preschool age. A number of factors continue to place the grandparent in this prominent position. Primary among them is the fact that both parents are expected to work full time, while places in nurseries and kindergartens are in short supply. A second important consideration is the different retirement ages for men and women. Grandmothers, in particular, retire in their early fifties, just at the point when their sons and daughters are having young children in need of care. Finally, although neither the grandfather nor the mother-in-law carries the awesome authority each wielded in the traditional Chinese family, they have acquired a new status and prestige as the victims and teachers of "bitterness." Among the most cheerful people we met in China were retired workers and peasants, most of them now grandparents. For whatever reasons, the sense of being direct beneficiaries of the Communist regime or the traditional caution of the elderly, the grandparents expressed devotion to the principles of the regime and to Mao Tse-tung. Very often, when we commented on the pleasantness of a living area or apartment we were visiting, it would be a grandmother or grandfather who, with beaming face and great animation, would exclaim, "Thanks to Chairman Mao." We were, unfortunately, not able to assess the degree to which grandparents are also seen as continuing the ideologically unsavory traditions of religious activity and family rituals connected with birth, marriage, and death.

The grandmothers we saw seemed generally nurturant. Often

they are described by parents and teachers as overindulgent, and the emotional attachment between grandmother and grandchild may indeed be quite strong. One may speculate that to hear from a beloved caretaker tales of the bitter past and the wondrous present made possible by Mao's leadership is not likely to be without effect on the child's psychological development. The grandmother in contemporary Chinese society may play a significant part in maintaining the almost religious commitment we observed to Maoist ideals and to Mao himself, but there may well be, particularly in more rural areas, as many grandparents who try to continue the old ways.

Parental Roles. One of the clearest impressions gained in our brief and scattered observations and interviews was that fathers took an active part in household chores and child care. They did not, however, seem to carry a fully equal share; the mother and, when present, the grandmother were clearly doing more with the children. In one family the wife made a little speech saying that the husband is stronger and should do more of the housework. He then made a little speech on how important it is to educate the children and to take them to places they have learned about in school. He reported taking his daughter to the People's Park, taking her to a shopping center that is open late at night, and to other public places. It was interesting that there was at least a semblance of expression of dissatisfaction with the division of labor in this family on the part of the wife.

Two factors undoubtedly serve to reinforce the somewhat active role taken by fathers in the home—the official ideological commitment to equality of the sexes and the exigent demands of reality. With both parents working, often on different schedules, housework and child care get done by whoever is there when something is needed. On a number of occasions when we asked who in the family did the cooking, the answer was, "Whoever gets home first for a particular meal."

Other agents of upbringing in the home. One pattern we had expected to see but did not often observe was the involvement of older siblings, or for that matter, older children generally, in the care of the young. Again, we must be guarded in our conclusions because of the limited nature of our observations and because other observers have reported the common occurrence of sibling care. Perhaps we were seeing a part of the culture in change. For one thing, families with many children are not as common as they once were; as a result, when one child is young there is not likely to be another child in the family old enough to take much responsibility for caregiving. Second, as we have seen, once a child enters kindergarten or regular school, he acquires many responsibilities for work and social service both within and outside the school. Third, and perhaps most important, the official line does not always support traditional family values. "Serving the people" seems to carry an emphasis on helping the peasants, workers, and soldiers rather than an emphasis on strengthening and protecting the initial family.

On the other hand, we were struck by the degree and variety of social support given the Chinese family. We have written about the elderly and their place as general overseers and caretakers of children. Additional sources of support to the family are home visits on the part of teachers and health personnel. Several of the parents with whom we talked spoke warmly and gratefully of the help these personnel gave them in caring for and bringing up their children. Teachers apparently also share some of the responsibilities of parents. At a boarding kindergarten in Peking, for example, the teachers told us, "To lessen the burden for parents, we do the haircutting and the laundry."

Child behavior and child-rearing practices

The most difficult task we could have set ourselves was to find out how Chinese parents actually treated their children. Nevertheless, we believe our interviews and observations on this score have some value. To begin with, what a parent says in reference to his child is revealing even when it is not true. Furthermore, it is difficult to change one's behavior toward one's child because company is present, and even more difficult to change the behavior of the child himself. Finally, we got the feeling in a number of conversations with parents, including both those whom we visited at home and others whom we met informally in our travels, that as we began to talk with them about their children we were penetrating, if only in a slight degree, the bounds of a purely formal relationship, and learning something of the reality of their lives.

From these sporadic glimpses, two consistent impressions emerged. The first was merely an extension, or perhaps the root, of what we saw in the group settings we visited: in their homes, as in their kindergartens and primary schools, young Chinese children were extraordinarily poised and well behaved. There was very little distress at the arrival of strangers; on the contrary, the children often took the initiative in greeting us, starting conversations, exploring intriguing objects such as cameras, or showing us toys. As soon as the interview began a child would begin to amuse himself quietly with his own books and toys, usually without any instructions from the mother, and seldom requiring the parent's attention.

The second impression was also consistent with our observations in other settings. Like the teaching personnel, parents and grandparents were predominantly warm and positive in their relations with the children. Moreover, in contrast with the usual absence of physical touching in schools, there was a substantial amount of body contact between children and adults at home; fathers as well as mothers and grandparents often held children on their knees for shorter or longer periods. When not in physical contact, the parents often smiled at the children and exchanged warm glances with them. It was clear by the usual markers that the adults we saw enjoyed their children and grandchildren.

During the visits themselves we observed no acts of negative disciplinary control, and indeed, no behavior on the part of the children, other than restlessness, that might have required it. From the interviews we got few reports of bad behavior and even fewer instances of punishment. Several mothers mentioned difficulties with getting the children to go to bed, or complained of their desire to play instead of engaging in educational activities (such as looking at books or listening to political programs on the radio). In reply to a question about what she did if her children misbehaved, one mother of two daughters (ages five and nine) replied that the older one was never naughty but occasionally the younger one was. Sometimes the two sisters quarreled; in that case, the mother asked the little one whether the elder was right in what she said about the reason for the quarrel. There was no question that the older daughter was regarded as quite exemplary and that she was given great responsibility.

Another mother gave the following account:

> My daughter, who is five years old, told me she had been bad in school. Her teacher had been speaking to her, and she could not control herself and giggled at the teacher. I told her she should not do this, but then one day she said to me that it had happened again. Now I became worried. I said to her, "You must learn to have discipline over yourself. If you do not, you will not be accepted into the Little Red Soldiers and the Red Guard."
>
> When the teacher came to our home for her visit, I was sure she would complain about my daughter. But she didn't say anything about it, so I brought it up. The teacher said, "Yes, she is very lively, but I am not worried. She is a good girl and she will learn."

From such comments by parents, never disconfirmed by what we saw, we gained the impression that although parental standards for good behavior were rather exacting they seldom required enforcement, since children generally lived up to or even exceeded expectations. When a minor deviation did occur, it usually took only a gentle hint or reminder for the child himself to begin to mend his ways. Of course, we had no way of assessing the frequency or occasions of more severe reprimands and had to remember the reports of child-beating in China, at least up to 1957.

To a remarkable degree education in preschool and school presents a model for appropriate behavior in the home as well. Often the same lesson takes different forms. For example, several times in various kindergartens and primary classes, the children were exposed to the following paradigm: a child has an old shirt or coat or bookcase or toy, he is ashamed to have his classmates see it, and he asks his parents for a new one. A mother or father or grandparent or PLA uncle speaks to the child, describing or showing the same or a similar object in its impoverished version "in the time of bitterness." For example, the child is given his grandfather's threadbare coat or the PLA man describes the attire of the Eighth Route Army and displays his own shirt, patched and resewn by his own hands. The child immediately understands, renounces interest in the new possession, and eagerly repairs the old.

In the last scene of this recurring story, the renovated object and its renovator are receiving the enthusiastic attention and approval of peers and adults. This paradigm reappears in story books, posters, accounts by parents, children's songs and dances, and testimonials by leaders and rank and file of the Little Red Soldiers. We seemed to be hearing a systematic delineation of what constituted a problem and what constituted a proper solution to it; Chinese children are asked to learn the established pattern.

That such lessons are not without effect is underlined by the spontaneous comment of one of our hosts as we were watching some kindergartners performing (for the third or fourth time, with minor local variations) what we came to call "The Big Apple" (the happy moral: give the big apple to others; keep the little one for yourself). Our Chinese host leaned over and said, "You know, as a result of this song my little son changed his behavior toward his baby sister; he began to be very kind to her." At the time we wondered about the sincerity of the remark, but as we came to know Chinese children and families better we grew somewhat less skeptical. The continuity of affection and high expectation of conforming behavior that the young child experiences in both family and school, the endless repetition, the support and pressure of peers, the recurring exposure to cognitively unambiguous, universally approved models of good behavior—these indeed appeared to result in high levels of competence and conformity.

Developmental changes in training and behavior

When he enters primary school, the Chinese child, like the child in other cultures, is expected to take increased responsibility for himself. If he has not attended kindergarten, special attention may be needed, to insure sufficient training in self-reliance, for example, to help him take a measure of responsibility for after-school activities, especially if there are no grandparents at home to oversee his activities. At home and in school, the child is exposed both to repeated exhortations to service and self-reliance and to stories of young folk heroes who have exhibited these traits. The continuity between little good deeds and heroic deeds is stressed. Small steps toward self-reliance can be the start of a long journey, to paraphrase an oft-cited saying of Mao Tse-tung.

Parents still provide a framework of supervision for the primary school child, often backed up by grandparents and retired workers for the urban child, but school assignments and peer-group sharing of out-of-school study give opportunities for a measure of experience in self-control and social control. So too does participation in the Little Red Soldiers and, later, the Red Guards. Structured sessions of self-criticism take on seriousness in primary school and become much more institutionalized in middle school. We were able to secure very little information on friendship patterns, but pairs of preadolescents and adolescents, *always* of the same sex, are a common sight as one travels along China's streets and roads. Since children tend to stay with the same classroom group for years, continuities in friendship are supported.

Many urban children go to the countryside or to other extended work assignments after junior middle school, when they are fifteen years old (they have typically made short work trips to the countryside earlier on). The junior-middle-school graduates, we were told, would be assigned relatively nearby, while those who have finished senior middle school might be sent to more distant provinces. One middle school in Shanghai had a map showing the places where its students had been assigned, and these included fifteen provinces and one autonomous region.

From the amount of untranslated discussion that occurred when we raised questions about such assignments, it would appear that there are differences of opinion as to this policy and its consequences. Some of our informants stressed that the adolescent could return to visit the family at least once a year, others, that young people had to be willing to go where they were needed. We were even told that if the family could make a strong case for keeping a child at home, it was possible to make such an arrangement; and an only child could stay with his parents instead of going to the countrysiae if he wished to do so. But if the child preferred to go despite his parents' desires, the authorities would support his desire to "serve the people." In Peking we were told that students who finished middle school before they were seventeen would be kept at the school as helpers or allowed to take special studies because they were too young to be sent to the distant countryside.

The family and the school

There is a great deal of communication between Chinese teachers and parents, especially at the younger-age points of transition into new school settings. Some communication takes place informally, when parents deliver young children to the school or pick them up, but there are a number of more formal modes, usually initiated by the schools. These include meetings for parents, apparently most often held early in the school year or at the end of the year, visits from teachers to the homes of the students, and small notebooks that pass back and forth between school and home, variously referred to by our interpreters as "communication books" or "connection notebooks." The exchange between school and home in China, apparently so much more fluid and continuous than that in the United States, may again show the effects of the more stable and tighter organization of Chinese neighborhoods. Caretaking institutions generally seem not to be separated from one another as definitely as they are in the West.

At the nursery and kindergarten level, children are taken to school and picked up by their parents or other adults, so there is frequent opportunity for contact between teachers and the child's family. In general, such contacts seem to involve brief exchanges of information about the child's health, about major events affecting the child in the family, or about problem behaviors or attitudes of the child in the school setting. If there are urgent problems such as acute illness or injury of the child, we were repeatedly told, teachers will telephone the parents. Since at least one of the parents is normally at work when the child is in kindergarten, a call to the workplace is probably feasible; we did not see telephones in any of the homes we visited.

A primary-school teacher at the July First Commune in the suburbs of Shanghai was present during one of our interviews with parents. The teacher sat on the edge of the bed, the mother on a low stool just in front of her. On several occasions the teacher leaned forward and put an arm around the mother's shoulders. They smiled and joked together. We thought they might have been girlhood friends, and asked how long they had known each other. It turned out that the teacher had not grown up in this village, but had gotten to know the family when their little girl (now ten) entered the first grade and the teacher had made her first family visits.

Our information on home–school contacts at the primary school level comes largely from first-grade teachers in the Shanghai Experimental School and from the reports of parents and grandparents. The first-grade teachers said that prior to the start of school they visit all the families of children listed for assignment to their classes, either on the parents' day off from work or in the evening. In these visits the teachers reported that they seek to learn about the family situation—who the primary caretakers are, their general views about child care, the adequacy of space and other physical conditions for homework—and the nature of the child's friendship ties and the "strengths and weaknesses" of the child. If the child has gone to a kindergarten in the local area, the first-grade teacher will also visit the kindergarten to learn about the child. We were not told of the use of written records in this regard.

Children seen as having "weaknesses" are given special attention by the teacher and special coaching through "cooperation with the parents." We have a hunch (no more) that children who are thought by parents to be severely "weak" or deviant are kept at home. One of the weaknesses ascribed to first-grade children who have not attended kindergarten is that they have been spoiled by their grandmothers. Such children are seen by at least some teachers as lazy and not independent. When the teacher makes the diagnosis of overindulgent grandmother, she apparently "explains" to the grandmother that she must expect the child to be independent and must be firm. Teachers differed in their opinions about children who had not gone to kindergarten; some saw them as needing extra help in adjusting to the disciplined environment, while others thought that children with experience of kindergarten were harder to control in class because they were so "lively." Our observations suggest that the strong position taken against "spoiling" in Chinese youth and women's periodicals before the Cultural Revolution, when publication stopped, is carried out; the child is indeed prepared for a somewhat spartan future built on cooperation with and respect for others.

Our Shanghai teachers reported that after the start of primary school parents are brought together for an evening meeting to receive an orientation to the program planned for the class. Parents are expected to be familiar with the child's homework and thereby to have some idea of what goes on at school. At the middle-school level (and, here most of our data come from Peking School #31) parents' meetings are held at the beginning and the end of each term. First the parents are given an overview by the responsible persons, and then the principal teacher in each classroom discusses the teaching plan for the whole term. The teachers make clear the demands that will be made on students, apparently so that parents will reinforce those demands. Parents are also invited to the schools just after the students return from their month of work in the "countryside." Since the class goes together, the parents come to the classroom to learn about the experiences of the group during this period. It was not clear how much these reports involved discussion with individual families.

At Peking #31 we were told that teachers always visit the homes of children who come to the school when their families move into the district. They may also visit to "congratulate" families of children who make exceptional progress or who are invited to join the Red Guards. And they may visit the families of students who "are very quiet or are unable to complete their work," in order to find out the nature of the problem. Absences are checked on by student leaders rather than by the teachers, but if there are behavioral problems and the students do not change after warning, the teachers go to the homes and ask for help.

During the summer vacation, study activities are organized largely by the students, meeting at the home of a student leader. The teachers periodically visit such groups to see how they are getting along.

As is evident from the foregoing account, we feel the influence of school on family in China is far more potent than the influence of family on school. We heard such statements as, "education must be done by school, society, and family" and "Children are not the property of their parents; they are the successors to the revolution." In general, kindergarten is apparently seen as a more desirable experience than exclusive family rearing although everyone agreed that children brought up at home can still get a basic education, especially if the parents and grandparents are helped by the local health workers and Revolutionary Committee members.

No parent or grandparent suggested to us that schools ought to operate differently from the ways they do; no parent or grandparent suggested that teachers were unfair or unsympathetic. Parents were, of course, speaking in the presence of interpreters and members of the local Revolutionary Committee, but we felt that, by and large, the parents we spoke with accepted the competence of teachers and the appropriateness of the programs in the schools.

Teachers and school administrators, on the other hand, occasionally mentioned inadequacies in both home rearing and in teacher performance. When a teacher is unsympathetic to a child and fails to understand the child's needs (especially at the middle-school level), other students—especially members of the Red Guard—and teachers apparently may mobilize support for the student and "help" the teacher to be less critical and more accepting. Self-criticism is said to be an important part of the educational regime, and may afford a better impetus for change than would hostile commentaries by parents and grandparents. We were also told that a student could put up a "big character poster" against a teacher who is in the wrong. How often this happens at present, and with what consequences, we could not ascertain.

The schools depend on older people for help but, we were told, intergenerational education is a two-way street. The young are characterized as having "more culture," and thus being able to explain many things to the older generation, among them politics. Since the child begins learning about political thought from the time of entrance into school, he has a considerable store of precepts and mottos by the time he reaches middle school. In classical dialectical synthesis, the old educate the young about the past and the young educate the old about the future.

Family supports and constraints

As an agency of child rearing and child socialization, the Chinese family seems, on short acquaintance, to be better connected with other parts of the culture than is the American family. The adult members of the Chinese family receive both guidance and services from the schools, local Revolutionary Committees, and local health workers. Although we have relatively little information on the ways local committees help parents, we were told that if parents or grandparents neglect to supervise their children, then the neglect is looked into by local committees. We were also told that in the cities there are health workers, with training somewhat like that of barefoot doctors, who are available to help parents and grandparents to care for their children "morally as well as physically." And our own interviews and observations would suggest that informal sources of support from neighbors, the extended family, and retired workers are even more common than formal assistance.

Yet if we remember the power of parents over children in traditional Chinese family life, no change the Communist regime has brought about is more startling than the apparently diminished power of parents. Of course, the traditional family had the power of controlled inheritance, a power now available only in dramatically diminished form. Contemporary Chinese parents are able to indulge themselves in full enjoyment of the infant child a little less and to determine what the older child's primary activities will be a great deal less than in the past. Many of the institutional forms of support for the family in fact reduce the influence of the parents. Nurseries and kindergartens in factories and communes, while giving the parents help with child rearing, at the same time take away some of what were formerly prerogatives of the parents. There is, as well, substantial group pressure on parents to see that their children have the right attitudes.

But the principal challenge to the parents' primacy as agents of child rearing comes from the demands of work and political activity. Our impression was that especially urban Chinese families are subject to many kinds of separations of husband and wife and of parents and children. In most families both parents are in the labor force full time, sometimes on different shifts. Usually a night or two a week are spent in political study. A parent may be away from home for extended periods because of work assignments—a subsidiary plant might be established in another community or an industry may be shifted from one area to another—or political rehabilitation in the countryside. And of course, the major disruption of the traditional family that takes place when urban "educated youth" are sent to the countryside is one of the most striking indicators of the recent transformation of the urban Chinese family.

Thus, the major question we ask about the contemporary

Chinese family as an agent of socialization concerns the extent to which its influence over the child, and perhaps even its integrity as a childrearing system, are being transformed by the demands of the larger society. The modifying forces are powerful and have already had some dramatic effect. For example, the once unassailable claims of filial piety, and the domination of the young wife by the husband's mother, are visible only in pallid vestiges, such as the right of aging parents to be supported by their children. The new attitudes are reflected in the reply of a sixty-three-year-old grandmother to the question of whether children should ever marry persons of whom their parents would not approve: "Marriage is a matter for the younger generation; parents should not interfere." She went on to say that a son should choose whom he wants as a wife, despite the fact that the wife may well become a member of the mother's household. It is crucial to learn how representative this modification of the traditional attitudes is.

Any answer to this question must take into account the fact that the question is posed not for families in general but for the Chinese family in particular. As in other modernizing cultures, there may be a tendency for the father–mother–children group to become stronger as the ties to grandparents and the larger kinships are lessened in strength. But Chinese extended-family ties have always been exceptionally strong and, so far as we could see, they continue to remain strong today. Nor are long hours of labor, or frequent and extended separation of parents from each other or from their children new in Chinese history. Wars, sickness, overseas migration, famine—all have brought with them the fracturing of households and the separation of family members. And the usual solution too is a familiar one: someone else, typically a grandparent, steps into the breach. Given the historical experience of Chinese families, it seems unlikely that the current set of disruptive pressures, different only in direction, will critically weaken the familial fabric that binds the generations in China, particularly when these pressures, rather than destroying the capacity of communities and individuals to survive, have served to give them greater strength and dignity.

The fact of continuity as a context for radical change in China raises the question of how much of what we saw of child rearing, especially in the family, is truly different from the past? How much is Maoist, how much simply Chinese? Given our incompetence as historians of Chinese culture, our delegation could not properly begin to answer this question. Extensive observations and interviews in one or more communities of overseas Chinese would be needed, as would a fuller, more leisurely, and more systematic account of the details and texture of family life on the mainland. One slight glance can only provoke a greater interest in close study of the present Chinese family.

We must close our discussion of the Chinese family as we opened it, with a reminder of the pitifully small number of families from whom our information was obtained, the highly selective sample, and the fact that, in our observations and interviews, we were never alone with parents and children.

Infants less than a year old lie in a factory "feeding station." Their mothers, working nearby, will nurse them during breaks in the work shift.

The very old and the very young are often together in China. The men, all over seventy, who tend the fruit trees also tend the boy.

Two-year-olds in a nursery class. Most of the toys they use are visible in the picture; the crowding is representative of our observations; the color and variety of the clothing contrasts with the plainness of adult clothes; and the capitalist on the right has a toy in each hand.

Feet on floor, hands in lap, bibs in place, toddlers form the semicircle for instruction that will be used for a number of years.

3. NURSERIES IN CHINA

*The children are taught to love Chairman Mao, the Great Social-
ist Motherland, the Communist party, the workers, peasants, and
soldiers, and productive labor.*

—Capital Iron and Steel Factory Nursery, Peking,
November 19, 1973

The term *nursery-age child* has a relatively uniform definition
in China, as do the succeeding educational categories of kindergarten, primary, and middle-school child. The nursery-age child
is typically between about two months and about three years of
age. The earlier age is more fixed than the latter, for many Chinese mothers take an eight-week maternity leave. Even if the
mother decided to return to work before the end of her leave, it
is likely, although we cannot say for sure, that the nursery would
not accept a baby younger than two months old.

In settings that have a conveniently located kindergarten, the
child is usually transferred to the kindergarten when he is about
three years old. In the one setting we saw without an accessible
kindergarten, nursery- and kindergarten-age children were housed
in the same building, though children of different ages were
cared for by different members of the staff. The Chinese treat age
as a serious matter and tend to keep children in homogeneous age
groupings, with ranges of about six to ten months between the
oldest and youngest child in each group. In factory settings we saw
a further differentiation, between toddlers and very young infants,
who are in "feeding rooms" or "feeding stations" close to the
mothers' places of work. Since most infants are said typically to
be nursed until their first birthday, it is necessary to keep the
nursing child close to its working mother.

53

Our observations do not permit a firm conclusion, but our impression is that most nurseries care for children on a daily basis. A member of the family brings the child to the nursery when the mother goes to work and picks the child up in the late afternoon when the parents leave for home. In some settings, usually the rural communes, a member of the family picks the child up for lunch and returns him to the nursery when the parents return for the afternoon work period. In rural areas, during heavy work sessions, the child's stay in the nursery can last from six in the morning to six at night. Factories apparently have eight-hour shifts; and nurseries in three-shift factories usually stay open round-the-clock, with the baby staying in the nursery for the time the parent is working. Several officials told us that flexible scheduling is meant to fit all the various work shifts of parents, so that some infants or toddlers might only sleep at a nursery. The least common arrangement in China is reported to be the boarding nursery, where the infant remains in residence from Monday morning until either late Saturday afternoon or Sunday morning, and is with the family on Sunday. This arrangement typically, perhaps exclusively, occurs in urban settings where the parents are cadres or government officials who are away from home for long periods and where there is no grandparent or other kin available to provide home care.

The settings visited

One or more members of the delegation visited a total of nine nursery settings, four for very brief periods lasting less than thirty minutes and five for longer periods ranging from one to several hours. The settings were a nursery at a rural commune in the suburbs of Canton (November 17), two factory nurseries in Peking (November 19 and 20), two street nurseries in Peking (November 22), a factory-run nursery in Sian (November 27), two nurseries attached to workers' residences in Shanghai (November 30 and December 1), and nurseries in a suburban commune outside Shanghai (December 3).

Although there were obvious differences among the settings, which will be described later, there were a small number of important similarities that can be listed quickly. Generally, the children were in small groups of homogenous age with one adult for every six to seven infants. There were very few toys available for play. The playpens and the cots in which the children slept were close together and rarely contained toys. An infant had, at the most, one toy that seemed to be his very own; often it was clutched tightly in hand. Rarely did we see toys on the floor, but usually there were a few toys sitting on shelves or windowsills. We were told that toys are important for children but that nurseries cannot afford to purchase many. We were told by another teacher that since infants sleep a lot, they prefer not to play, and adults accommodate to the infant's "basic nature." When asked, "When does an infant begin to think?" one teacher replied that eight months marked the commencement of thought, as evidenced by reliable recognition of mother and caretaker, and by imitation. Such a belief might lead caretakers to be relatively unworried about interaction with or stimulation of the infant in the first months of life; our observations were certainly in accord with such a conclusion.

Caretakers do not generally encourage nursery-age children to be freely mobile or to play alone for long periods of time. They also discourage infants one year or older from crawling (remember, the floors were cold and many nursery rooms were small), walking about freely, or choosing a preferred solitary activity. We typically saw groups of six to twelve children between one and three years of age sitting in circles, standing on porches, walking in lines, or involved in group games. Children under three years of age, at least in the presence of strange visitors, were quiet and affectively subdued—in some contrast to the kindergarten children, who were verbal, expressive, and socially responsive. The nursery children loosened up after a while, of course, but the younger ones especially never showed the gaiety and liveliness of kindergartners.

The infants were usually well bundled up, for in Peking and Sian the temperature was between forty and fifty degrees and the nurseries were either unheated or heated by small coal stoves. Each child wore several layers of heavily padded clothing. The trousers of both boys and girls had a slit so that the child could urinate or defecate into a round pot without pulling down his pants. Although the practice prevents the chilling of thighs and legs on a cold day, the child may experience a distinctly cool sensation when he bends over on a windy day or scoots down a metal slide.

The children were generally docile and conforming, displaying little of the restlessness, rough and tumble play, grabbing of property, or the pushing and striking of peers that are common in American homes and nursery schools. Finally, to the American eye untutored in the marks of Chinese individuality, there was dramatically less variability in temperament and style of behavior among these very young Chinese children than among American children of the same age. Again and again, we made note of the calm, the orderliness, and the apparent uniformity of the young children of China.

A typical day

Nurseries conform to a daily schedule more structured than one often sees in American centers. Since many staff apparently do not believe that adult–child playful interaction or toys are critically important for babies, active indoor play is minimal and in most places absent. All activity is typically initiated by the adult teacher. Teachers seem to prefer to change specific activities every minute or two and change the theme or location of play every fifteen or twenty minutes. Each teacher seemed consciously or unconsciously to try to avoid boredom by changing the content of a routine often. These changes included alternating between indoor and outdoor activities.

A typical day begins with a health check to determine if any of the children have colds, fevers, or infections. For the babies this is followed by feedings spaced throughout the day, by napping, by informal play in cribs or walkers, floor play, and sometimes being walked and held by caretakers. The toddlers go from breakfast to simple supervised activities; then they have brief classes; then they go outdoors for play, games, exercises, or walks. Lunch is followed by a nap, after which the toddlers are served a snack. They play out of doors, or have vigorous indoor play if the weather is bad. Boarding toddlers eat an early supper, enjoy quiet play, and go to bed at around six-thirty or seven. Children on a day schedule go home for supper and the night.

The purposes behind Chinese nurseries and kindergartens were said to be to help liberate mothers for the working forces, to ease the burdens of working parents, to promote the all-around moral, intellectual, and physical development of the children, and to educate children so that they might become skillful and disciplined, and able later to assume adult responsibilities as "successful revolutionary workers."

Infants were described to us as dependent, helpless, and relatively inactive, and they appeared to be cared for without great effort to stimulate their sensory and intellectual development; early care is centered on careful feeding and hygiene. When babies become toddlers and nursery-age children, however, their education becomes a matter for curricular planning "according to their ages," say their teachers. Near the end of his second year, the toddler begins to see the large, colorful posters that introduce him to Mao's thought; he first hears the stories of the heroes in simple form for a few minutes each day. The toddler also learns to handle simple art materials, to name common objects and categories, to engage in personal hygiene routines, and to participate in songs, dances, and games. He learns to play cooperatively and helpfully with other children, to control impulsive behavior, to follow routines, and to participate in a rigorous outdoor life of games, races, exercises, and use of playground equipment. Moral education is stimulated through songs and dances celebrating the five loves—Chairman Mao, workers–peasants–soldiers, the Communist party, the Great Socialist Motherland, and physical labor.

The staff

Staff members are almost never college graduates. They are typically either educated females who have had some middle-school education or less educated women, perhaps selected on the basis of temperament, experience with children, and fondness for infants. We saw no male teachers in any nursery and assume that they are rare. Here, as elsewhere, the strategy appears to be to recruit suitable people, who are then trained as apprentices on the job. The ratio of formal and theoretical training to practical experience of new teachers in China is dramatically lower than the corresponding ratio in the West.

The typical child–adult ratio is about six to one for infants under one and a half years and about eight or ten to one for children one and a half to three years. The staff was generally nurturant, nonpunitive, soft-spoken, and by any measure concerned with the children. We saw only one instance of physical punishment of any kind and only one occurrence of a strong reprimand; if a child had to be corrected—and the occasions were rare—the teacher quickly moved to the scene of the violation and gently removed the child or moved a part of his body. On occasion, something was said to the child; however, the socialization intrusions were usually nonverbal. For example, if a line of children was supposed to be standing against a wall and a particular child moved a foot from the wall or began to lean on a peer, the teacher would gently move the child to his proper posture or to another part of the line. The child typically accepted this minimal press and conformed to the teacher's implied request.

The child in his environment

In Shanghai we saw a nursery that consisted of several different buildings with large rooms and quite a bit of outside play space. We also saw a setting that was the hall of an old building, with two dozen cots lined against one wall and about three to four feet of space remaining in the narrow hallway. Even in our limited experience, there was great variety in facilities for nurseries.

Vignettes from five nursery sites

It may be helpful to describe in some detail observations made in five settings where one or more of us stayed at least an hour:

the street nursery in Peking, the two nurseries attached to workers' residences in Shanghai, the small nursery attached to a work team on a rural commune outside Shanghai, and in a factory.

A FEEDING STATION   We saw few children in the first year of life in institutional settings. Whether for administrative or theoretical reasons—one could almost hear our Chinese hosts wondering why grown men would be interested in infants—we got only the briefest glimpse of the first period of group care for Chinese children. In one factory, we saw a "feeding station." A large cold room was almost filled by a platform on which were two perfect rows of about fifteen babies each. Spaced at almost exact intervals of three feet, the babies lay immobile on their backs. No crib guards were necessary; the children were so heavily bundled that they could neither roll nor turn (we wondered how they were kept in place during the hot months). Suspended above the lines of babies, about four feet away from them, were lines of toys—teething rattlers, apparently—with one such toy directly over each baby.

We spoke briefly with the two caretakers or nurses in charge of the feeding station. The babies spend their mother's work shift in the room, as we had been told before, and are fed by their mothers during regular breaks. When we asked about routines, particularly about how often the babies were picked up and played with (each nurse had a child in her arms throughout our short stay), we were told, "If a child cries, we comfort him; otherwise, they lie on the platform." For children in the first year, there seemed to be no perceived need for further stimulation or for either cognitive or social games during the eight hours of their stay at the feeding station.

THE PEKING STREET NURSERY (RENMIN)   This boarding nursery houses eighty children and twenty-eight staff members in a house with several small buildings and about 400 square feet of outside play space. Four of us spent part of a morning observing there and two of us a whole day. A small number of non-Chinese children, whose parents were members of the diplomatic corps in Peking, attended this nursery. The children ranged in age from one and a half to four years and were divided into four groups (one and a half to two, two and a half, three, and over three years of age). The typical day was as follows: 6 A.M. awakening, followed by a physical checkup, exercise and at 7:00 washing; 8:00 breakfast; 8:30–9:00 unstructured activity; 9:00–11:00 classes including games, naming objects, dancing and exercises; 11:00 washing; 11:30 lunch; 12:00–2:30 sleep; 3:00 snack followed by free activity; 6:00 supper; 7:00 bed. We were told that the formal twenty-minute classes specifically aimed at stimulating moral and intellectual development occurred in the morning after breakfast.

In one class of two and a half year olds the teacher was showing a picture to a group of thirteen children seated in a circle. A child was to say what the picture represented. The task seemed too difficult for some of the children; they were distractable and talked to one another. About half of the group continued to pay close attention throughout the lesson. The teacher terminated the class and took her children outside to an adjacent play area of about 200 square feet that had a slide, a small roundabout, and a rocking boat, among which the children distributed themselves rather evenly. In a few minutes three different age groups with three teachers were playing in this outside area, the other two having come from a different part of the complex. During a twenty-minute observation we saw only one act of direct aggression and two acts of gentle pushing displayed by twenty-seven Chinese children, in contrast with five acts of aggression or pushing for the three non-Chinese children in this play area. There were no requests for help and no crying. The children were allowed to wander in the play area freely, but no child wandered long without an occupation.

In another part of the nursery a group of thirty three-year-olds with three teachers was being shown how to shoot a small toy gun at a doll. The teacher first demonstrated how to hold and shoot the gun and then helped each child. Most of the children were apparently not fully engaged by the task, nor did they ex-

press visible excitement when the doll fell down, despite the fact
that the teacher praised them. As in our other observations, the
children patiently awaited their turns to play with the toy. Later,
outside, the teacher showed the children a toy Ping-Pong table
with players—which, we were told, they had not seen before—
explained how the toy worked, and placed it on the ground. None
of the thirty children who crowded closely around the toy touched
it or reached toward it, although many came close to it and all were
attentive. The teacher then brought out an electric airplane to
demonstrate but no one played with this toy. The teacher remarked that the purpose of showing these three toys was to famil-
iarize the child with Ping-Pong, airplanes, and guns, all of which
are salient objects in contemporary Chinese culture.

The teachers we saw moved easily around rooms and play
areas; if a group grew too large or noisy, a teacher appeared to
make an adjustment. The teachers kept the children continually
active and rarely did the children play on their own for more than
a few minutes. The children were lively in their play, yet remained
capable of immediate inhibition and restraint the moment an adult
so requested.

The teachers recognized that the games and dances practiced
in the nursery were simplified versions of the kindergarten activities. Hence children were being made familiar with the demands
the kindergarten would make on them when they moved on to the
next stage of their education.

The outstanding characteristics of the nursery included the
group nature of activities, the continual structuring by the teachers, and the attractive mixture of affective spontaneity and an
accommodating posture by the children. It was revealing to us
that, at lunchtime, the only children who needed help with the
food or special encouragement to eat were the few non-Chinese
children. Perhaps some sense of the remarkable control of young
Chinese children can be gained from our further observations on
the Ping-Pong toy. After the children had been watching the toy
raptly for a while, one of the teachers put a non-Chinese child
down from her arms. Without hesitation, he lunged for the new

toy, breaking through the circle of Chinese children and requiring recapture by his Chinese teacher. We saw almost no such impulsive movements from Chinese children of any age.

DAILY NURSERY IN SHANGHAI ATTACHED TO WORKERS' RESIDENCES   The nursery is run by a revolutionary committee attached to a workers' residential quarters in Shanghai. We were told that the neighborhood had nine revolutionary committees and four nurseries scattered throughout a residential area that serves 9,900 families. The nursery we visited is said to be open twenty-four hours a day, but most children are there during only one of the eight-hour work shifts. Most children arrive by five or six in the morning and leave late in the afternoon. For parents on a night shift, the nursery is open in the evening. We visited one of the four nurseries housed in an old, two-story building with many rooms. The nursing children were in feeding rooms close to where the mother worked and we did not see them. This building contained children between one and a half and six years of age and hence combined nursery and kindergarten age children, with a total stated child population of 190 served by nineteen teachers and their supporting staff. Since the children were in narrow age units and most had been enrolled at eighteen months of age, we had an unusual opportunity to observe cross-sectional age differences in behavior and temperament. In five small rooms along a single hall, we could, in a sense, see the development of children from eighteen months to four years.

The younger children were generally quiet and shy, and some did not make much response either to our presence or to the encouragement of their teachers. We observed one group of twelve children between eighteen and thirty months in a small room with two teachers. Each child held one toy, either a red ball or a doll. All were seated at a table and were quiet. As we approached, some began to show facial wariness and remained vigilant during our fifteen minutes in the room. During that period two of the twelve children—both boys—cried in what seemed to be a classic display of stranger fear.

Another room contained twenty two-and-a-half-year-olds and two teachers with no toys. The children were seated in a line against a wall. The teacher led them in a song about the importance of being healthy so one could serve the country. About eight of the children sang.

The two-and-a-half-year-olds in a third room were more lively. Some of them played on the wooden floor. Most were reserved, but one boy was relaxed and smiling. When we tried to play with the children, they were reluctantly willing, showing neither obvious anxiety nor enthusiasm.

The children in the first three rooms, all two and a half years or younger, were careful, quiet both of voice and body, and minimally social toward us. The nineteen children in the fourth room, between two and a half and three years of age, were quite a bit more spontaneous. None showed apprehension and most seemed at ease; they went on with their activities, aware of our presence but not distracted or apparently much subdued by it. In the fifth room, three-and-a-half- to four-year-olds were sitting in a circle. A girl was dancing in the middle of the room while twenty-six other children sat singing and watching her. The tone of the room and the character of the activity were much like those in the kindergartens we had been seeing. The difference between the expressive, well-organized, socially adept four-year-olds, and the immobile, shy, and almost expressionless toddlers just thirty feet down the hall was dramatic. We are relatively confident about the observation that Chinese children (at least in a setting like this one) change markedly in social responsiveness between one and a half and four years, but, alas, our evidence does not permit even useful speculation about the sources of the change.

DAILY NURSERY IN SHANGHAI (TS'AO-YANG) This daily nursery visited by two of us was located in another workers' residence area in Shanghai. The neighborhood was said to house thirteen nurseries and kindergartens serving 2,300 children and 5,400 families. We visited one of the nurseries, serving 350 children between one and a half and three and a half years of age, most of whom had been reared in a group setting since they were fifty-six days old. As with the previous nursery, the feeding rooms for children under one and a half were located in the factory close to where the mother worked. The nursery was newer and more spacious than the one just described. The unit consisted of several one-story buildings with large amounts of play area adjacent to each building, homogeneous age groupings, and a ratio of about nine children to one teacher.

The first group we observed contained twenty-seven children three to three and a half years of age with three teachers. The children were outside standing in three rows when we arrived. The teacher was demonstrating exercises which the children imitated. After about two minutes the teacher rang a bell and the children marched in place to the rhythmic ringing for thirty to forty seconds. The teacher then had the children line up against the wall of the building for a different game. She produced four paper crowns with rabbit heads, called four boys forward, put a paper crown on each, placed four chairs about 100 feet away and had the children hop to the chairs in a relay race. When these boys had completed their short journey, four girls repeated the race, then four boys, and so on. The peer spectators displayed considerable excitement, some hopping in place while the relay racers moved toward the chair. The group became moderately restless after a few minutes and when one boy gently shoved another the teacher quietly removed him to the end of the line.

In another area we observed seventeen children between two and two and a half years standing in a line on an outside porch containing no toys. Sixteen of the children rushed up to us as we walked on to the porch; only one girl remained in the background. The teacher then led the children from the porch onto a play area that contained a climbing gym and a rocking boat. Four children went to the gym, seven to the boat, and four were allowed to wander in the play area. After a few minutes a new group of twenty-two children two and a half to three years of age with one teacher marched into this area and formed a circle. In a few moments the original group of seventeen marched out of the play area, led by the teacher, with the timing of a rehearsed performance. The new group of twenty-two children formed a circle at their teacher's instruction. She gave a light plastic ball to one child and the ball was simply passed around the circle while the children clapped. When the ball returned to the original child twenty seconds later the teacher initiated a different activity. This time a girl was invited into the middle of the circle and the teacher and the rest of the class sang and made bodily gestures for twenty to thirty seconds. The teacher initiated a second round of ball passing. After this second episode of passing the ball the teacher invited the children to imitate her in a series of simple gestures and postures. She stopped this activity in a half minute and all the children dispersed in the play area. Most went to the large wooden boat, some began to play with the ball. As that play became active and lively the teacher came over and organized a structured activity by throwing the ball and having the children chase it. This sequence was the clearest demonstration we had of the tendency of nursery teachers to organize activities after relatively short bursts of time.

We moved to a different area and observed a group of twenty-seven three-and-a-half-year-old children in a large room with three teachers. Two children were singing in front of us while the remaining twenty-five sat quietly in a semicircle. The teacher played a song on a small piano while the children stamped their feet and sang for about twenty seconds. A new activity was introduced. Five boys and five girls stood up and marched in place in two lines singing a song about Little Red Soldiers who "exercise" so that they will be healthy and able to serve the country. Then six children, each holding a chair with a picture of a bus on the front, danced and sang while the remainder of the class sang a song about a bus driver. After thirty seconds the class sang a new song, followed by an activity in which a girl stood in the middle of the room and chose a partner from the seated group to dance with her while the other children clapped and sang. We cannot, of course, be certain how much of the schedule of varied activity was

planned for visitors but it was our impression that the visit was
not expected.

NURSERY SETTING IN A RURAL COMMUNE IN SHANGHAI (THE
JULY FIRST COMMUNE)   We visited a rural commune about
ten miles outside Shanghai said to contain 4,220 families in
eighty-eight production teams, with a nursery attached to each.
Thus each nursery should have served about fifty families. Each
was close to the residences of the families it served, sometimes
only a few yards away, and children of two to three years could
walk to the nursery alone. The nursery settings were small houses
with one or two caretakers and twelve to fifteen children; they
reminded us roughly of family day-care arrangements in the
United States. The commune also had a combined nursery and
kindergarten. As in nurseries we saw elsewhere, there were few
toys in these. One of us observed in one of the nurseries for about
ninety minutes; there were a dozen children between ten months
and four years of age and two staff members were present. The
detail of some observations made at July First may help to sketch
a picture of a Chinese nursery.

I asked permission to remain in the nursery rather than con-
tinue the tour and the Chinese leader of our group seemed, rather
hastily, to tell the caretakers ("nurses") that I would stay. I stood
in a corner of the room and looked down at the children. Each
child was bundled in jacket and pants, many had caps, and all (I
think) had knit wool stockings on under their slit pants. On each
toddler's coat was pinned or tied a handkerchief. One reached his
hand to me; I slowly squatted down, shook his hand, shook others'
hands. One after another offered his hand to be shaken. Each
nurse brought a baby-in-arms to have his hand shaken by me. I
was soon surrounded by a tight circle of toddlers pressing into
me with others just behind them. There was some pushing. The
old nurse was apparently nervous about the children touching me
or touching my belongings. The younger nurse organized the chil-
dren to sing several songs for me. They did, in soft voices but
with words at the tips of their tongues. I clapped when they were

through and there was a roar of laughter. I only then realized that
we were surrounded by a crowd of onlookers, men and women of
various ages, who appeared to be very curious and friendly.

While the children were singing, one little girl about three or
four years old in a red jacket (referred to hereafter as Red Girl)
started jumping. Then she tapped her feet to the next song in a
vigorous fashion. I tapped mine in imitation. The older nurse
stopped Red Girl when she did this a second time, yelling at her
and grabbing her. Red Girl stopped suddenly and ran her finger
into a crack in the concrete floor, flicking a little dirt up out of the
crack. The older nurse literally howled and slapped Red Girl's
hand. This was repeated twice.

I was still down at eye level with the pressing, pushing, eager
semicircle of children. (The younger nurse had given me a tiny
stool about eight inches high to sit on). The children vied for
space and a clear view of me by pushing each other. A very
bright-eyed boy of about three (the child who had first reached
out for me, whom I will call Blue Boy) stroked the pile lining on
the cuffs of my coat. He touched the coat in many places, then
touched my hands, looking into my face. Now he put his arm
around me and held on tight. He smiled, stared at me, said soft
words to me. The children around said something sounding like
"ay-yah"—probably a-yi, "auntie"—over and over to me. An-
other baby, just put in walker, burst into tears, and a man who
had been watching the scene leaned over and comforted it. Red
Girl suddenly darted out the door, through the courtyard onto the
street, and out of sight. The nurses cried out after her and seemed
very apprehensive; the older nurse went off after her.

I sang them "Clap Your Hands;" "This is the Way;" "Hickory-
Dickory Dock," and some others. They listened very attentively,
but did not imitate my sounds or actions. When I stopped, they
said several times in an insistent tone a word that I decided must
mean "another." I sang some more songs.

I stopped and drew a diagram of the room. As I drew, Blue
Boy chuckled and traced the lines of the drawing with his index
finger. Red Girl had returned; she and two others also traced the

lines. Then each in turn solemnly said what sounded like two or three words. I guessed that they might be telling me their names. By then the nurses were moving around more freely; each concerned with a baby, leaving the toddlers to me.

After I finished drawing the room diagram, I offered the paper and pen to the children. They looked inhibited and drew back a little, but eventually Red Girl drew, and then the rest got into a pushing contest over who would draw next. I tried to pass the paper and pen around. Finally, one of the taller children about four years old passed the pen, having gently removed it from my hand, to a little girl in back who had not been able to reach, and again to two other children in back.

The pushing got worse. Pocketing my pen and paper, I tried solfège singing. The children looked at me and smiled. I sang simple tones and intervals in an effort to get them to imitate me; only one child did and he only once.

Red Girl was holding the hand of a smaller child, who reached over and touched her face. Red Girl ignored that. She had a red plastic toy (a gadget, really; I did not see real toys in the room), which she gave another child near her. The other child moved over to the baby, who was being placed in a walker by the nurse who had been holding him. He grabbed the gadget. The adults all laughed, and then two or three adults pulled and hauled and seemingly teased these two children (child and baby) with the gadget—giving the gadget, taking it away and laughing, giving it back, and so on.

Now the baby had the toy; he mouthed it, waved it around. The toddlers started dispersing; it was time for them to go home for lunch.

I saw no toys or books in the nursery; there was, however, a small rattan storage unit that might have contained such supplies. There was no play equipment in the courtyard.

The children appeared to be very healthy, alert, friendly, curious.

The contrast between these notes and some of our other observations in nurseries is noteworthy; the children seem to have been under less stable control than in any of our other observations. We can only speculate about differences between city and country, differences in preparation of teachers, and (especially cautionary) differences in the circumstances of our observations. A long observation by a solitary visitor may have posed a critically different social problem for young Chinese children and for their teachers.

Reflections

Despite the variety in geography and structure, there were several major dimensions of similarity across the nursery environments and the children's behavior in these environments. There was an obvious preference by teachers for group over individual activity, a preference for song and dance over purely cognitive activities like reading books or language skills. There was adult restraint of what is apparently considered excessive spontaneity and motoricity, and, for an American, surprisingly little discernible variability among the children.

A few cautious generalizations can be made from these limited observations. For example, the uniform absence of many toys in the nurseries did not seem to produce obvious deleterious effects on what looked like spontaneity in the kindergarten children; what effects the lack may have on problem-solving ability is harder to assess. Or again, in the seven nursery settings we entered—foreigners strange in dress, color of skin, and facial topography—usually no more than a fraction of the children cried, and they briefly. Such apparently low levels of stranger anxiety indicate that the tendency to cry at unfamiliar events is brought under control at very early ages.

Our attention was repeatedly caught by the low level of motoricity or, perhaps, irritability in the Chinese children we saw. They were far less restless, less intense in their motor actions, and displayed less crying and whining than American children in similar situations. We were constantly struck by the quiet, gentle, and controlled manner of Chinese children and as constantly frustrated in our desire to understand its origins. Each of us, of course, has his theoretical prejudice, but all of us agreed that the gentleness and control of the children bore a resemblance to the gentleness and control of their teachers.

It is worth noting, however, what seems to be a marked reduction in holding and touching of children by adults when they go from home to school. When we asked one teacher if she picked up and held a crying child, she replied "newcomers cry sometimes; we try to lead them away from the group, console them, form relationships with them so that the children will know and love the teachers." On another occasion, a boarding-kindergarten teacher answered that she would sit at the bedside of a distressed and crying newcomer but would not hold him.

Obvious sex differences were small. Aggression was rare, and the usual excess of male over female aggression was not apparent. We were told by teachers in various settings that boys are a little more active and naughty than girls. There was little obvious sex segregation in activities or seating in the nursery.

One of the most significant questions left concerns the existence and character of differences between kindergarten children raised at home for the first three years of life and those who spend a significant part of the first three years in a nursery. Though the reports of kindergarten teachers varied, there was some consensus that nursery-reared children cried less, but might be harder to regulate at first, that grandmother-reared children were "self-centered," and that all such differences submitted relatively quickly to the discipline of the kindergarten. It may be that under the unique conditions in contemporary Chinese society the psychological differences between family-reared and group-reared infants and young children often seen in Western cultures are markedly diminished. Only further and more closely focused observations can test the proposition and, if it is confirmed, unravel the origins of the apparent uniformity.

With rapt attention, young Chinese children watch the workings of a new mechanical toy. The dramatic combination of concentration and tranquil control (look at the children's relaxed hands) repeatedly provoked our interest and puzzlement.

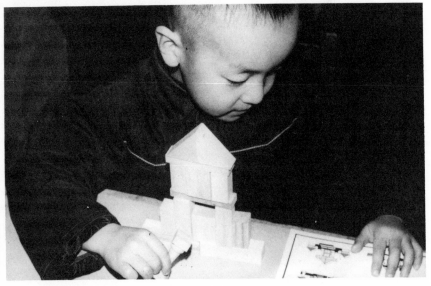

Copying and competence. With remarkable control and accuracy, a five-year-old constructs a block building. Like all of his colleagues whom we saw, he makes an exact copy from a model.

An early lesson in numbers. Three children match numerals to the pictures of radishes and then three others get a turn. We rarely saw an error in mathematics games.

Every school presented a song-and-dance program for us. We were astonished at the complexity of the dance routines and the theatrical commitment of even the youngest children.

In song and dance, a class enacts the conflict of the monitor who must decide whether to keep the large apple for herself or give it to a classmate. With the help of Mao's precepts, she makes the right choice.

4. THE CHINESE KINDERGARTEN

Before the Cultural Revolution, because of the revisionist line of Liu Shao-ch'i, our direction was not clear. After the Cultural Revolution, we taught the children according to the teachings of Chairman Mao.

—Briefing at East-Is-Red Kindergarten, Canton,
November 16, 1973

The experience of walking into a Chinese kindergarten is not one soon to be forgotten; the children line up near the gate or doorway and peer out, apparently eager for the first glimpse of the visitors. As soon as the first visitor is spotted the children begin to applaud excitedly and call out the conventional welcome, "Greetings, uncles and aunts." Then, often, one or two children step forward to take the hand of each visitor and pilot him to the briefing room. This experience is repeated each time one enters a new classroom. When visitors are expected the children are often held on "ready" for the moment the visitors enter the room, at which time the children burst into applause and, in carefully cadenced unison, repeat the greeting several times. Then, perhaps on a signal that we did not perceive, they stop and turn their complete attention back to their teacher. If the children are already engaged in an activity when the visitors enter the classroom, they stop instantly, applaud and chant their greetings, and then just as promptly go back to their work.

Although there are many elements of similarity from one school to another, we cannot comfortably make generalizations about "the Chinese kindergarten." All the schools we visited were in large urban areas, with the exception of kindergartens in three rural communes, and two of these were located only a short distance from a large city. Some schools we visited in the morning and others in the afternoon, and anyone with experience in early child development programs knows that time of day significantly affects what will be seen in a kindergarten. Kindergartens, like other Chinese educational settings, may be operated by factories, by street revolutionary committees, by rural communes, by regions of a city, by cities, or by the state. They may offer daytime care only or, more rarely, may board children from Monday morning until Saturday afternoon; there are some combined day and boarding schools. Some clearly served children of bureaucrats and Army officers, while others served children of workers or of peasants.

To let the reader know what kind of information we had at hand for the material presented here, there appears in the last pages of the report a list of all the facilities we visited. We will in the next pages present our perceptions of Chinese kindergartens more or less along the dimensions we would use to describe American kindergartens. We have tried to remain close to observation and to avoid speculation, but, as we have already noted, we found it impossible to doff our biases, personal and theoretical, altogether.

Physical plant

As is true in most countries, there is considerable diversity among the buildings that house kindergartens in China. Some of this diversity may be ascribed to the apparently rapid development of kindergartens after 1949. With one exception, a kindergarten program established in Yenan in 1939 and later moved to Sian, all the kindergartens we visited began operation in the late 1950s. Some were located in newly constructed buildings designed expressly to be either day or boarding kindergartens; many, however, were housed in physical facilities constructed for other purposes and adapted for young children.

The diversity was especially noticeable in the several communes we visited. For example, in a Canton commune, the nursery and kindergarten occupied the former landlord's villa. In a large commune near Shanghai, the kindergartens and nurseries were scattered over a large area and housed in small buildings that had formerly been homes or one-room stores. In a Sian commune, the kindergarten occupied two small, dark, and dirt-floored rooms of a new brick building. There was also considerable diversity in the cities. Although we visited only a small number of kindergartens in each city (there are said to be over two thousand nurseries and kindergartens in Peking alone), we saw a very broad range of physical plants. Workers' dormitories in a heavy machinery factory had been converted into kindergarten rooms in Canton. In a large school in Peking the kindergarten was housed in rooms of what had been worker's residences. We also visited a kindergarten in Peking with elegant rooms in what had formerly been the home of a well-to-do merchant.

Despite this variation, however, Chinese kindergartens had many common attributes. Only in one school was there central heating; in all the other schools there either was no heat or the minimal heat given off by a single charcoal stove. Windows in most of the schools were kept open and, except for the area immediately adjacent to the small stove, there was little difference between the temperature inside and that outside the building. Therefore the children are dressed warmly. They wear at least three layers of clothing: flannel or cotton clothing near the body, wool sweaters and leggings, and cotton-padded outer garments (Later in the winter heavy coats and cotton-padded shoes are apparently also worn.) There was no reason, then, to put on or take off clothing as the children came inside or went out to play—a boon for the teachers. Another method of adjusting to the temperature was to plan activities that keep the children warm. The teachers said that in the winter they frequently organized vigorous outdoor play, while in the summer they spend more time carrying out quiet activities.

Basic equipment. Against the almost complete homogeneity of dress that one encounters among Chinese adults, the little children stand out in sharp contrast. Kindergarten children are dressed in colored pants and jackets, with large and brightly colored hair ribbons as additional adornment for the girls. To step inside a kindergarten—an educational division that in China teaches children between the ages of three and seven—is to enter a world of color significantly more varied than the one outside. But the brightness and color come from the children themselves, not from furnishings and wall decorations; even in kindergartens, the physical environment tends to be spartan and austere. The rooms are lit by one or two open lightbulbs or open fluorescent lights. White-washed rather than painted walls are common. The floors are generally of dirt, wood, or stone; in only one of the schools we visited were the floors covered with rugs. On the front wall of most classrooms there is a picture of Chairman Mao, and side or rear walls may contain inspirational political posters. Rarely if ever does one see children's artwork on display. Almost every school had some musical instrument for group singing and dancing (small bellows organ, accordion, or occasionally a piano), and virtually every classroom had a flannel board or an easel upon which posters were tacked for lessons in language and politics. Typically each classroom had a small wall cabinet containing separate cubicles in which each child's cup was stored, and low on one wall there was always a row of hooks, each identified by some symbol or a number, from which hung the children's wash-cloths. Most classrooms contained small tables and chairs, several shelves, and a small chest for the storage of teaching materials.

None of the rooms had running water or toilet facilities. Toilets were located in another room of the building or in a room off the play yard. They were often of a design common in China and Japan—openings in the floor over which the children squat.

Equipment was very carefully used and seldom duplicated. In one relatively well furnished kindergarten in Peking, we arrived just as the children were getting up from their nap and were invited to observe the children making their beds and getting dressed. Although the children were partially undressed for their naps, there were no closets or cubby holes where the children could hang up or arrange their clothes. Instead, a row of chairs was neatly lined up against the window, each with the back of the chair away from the wall, and the clothes were laid on the chair backs. When each child got ready to dress himself, he turned his chair around, sat down on it, and put on the clothing he had taken off. Then when this ritual was complete, he picked up his chair and carried it into the next room where the same chair would be used for other teaching activities.

Depending upon the size of the school building and the number of children enrolled, the number of rooms devoted to activities other than teaching varies. Most schools have a conference room in which visitors are greeted, teachers confer and study, and parent–teacher meetings are said to be held. This large room may also serve as the locale for children's performances for visitors, although in many schools performances were presented in a separate room equipped with a stage and some musical instrument. Facilities for sleeping varied greatly. The most simple arrangement was sleeping boards that were lowered from the walls and covered with quilts. In other schools there were separate sleeping rooms where each child had a permanently assigned bed. Meals were generally brought to the children's classroom where, with adult help, class monitors serve the group. Depending upon the size of the school and whether it is boarding or day, the kitchen and laundry facilities might be quite extensive or very simple.

Available toys and games. The play materials we observed most frequently on kindergarten shelves or being used by children were pencils, colored pencils, scissors (very nicely designed for young children), watercolors and brushes, plasticine, table blocks (unpainted, painted, printed with pictures), battery powered and friction toys (trucks, cars, Ping-pong players, hens laying eggs), balls, small plastic, rubber, or metal cars, trucks, animals, and dolls, and cloth teddy bears. Other items we saw were paste, paper for folding and cutting, stencils, aluminum foil and other decorative papers for crafts, clay and clay boards, blackboards and colored chalk, drums, puzzles (usually small illustrated cube sets), miniature toy pianos (playable), jump ropes, hoops, plastic fruit, a homemade bus about two and a half feet square made of boxes, rubber dart guns, large blocks for floor play, and ten- to fourteen-inch dolls (only infrequently).

In performances given for visitors, the children used large blocks, puppets, chairs, or, in one instance, semaphore flags as props for their songs and skits. They also often wore costumes of the national minorities, sometimes quite elaborate and always very colorful, and makeup on their faces.

In one Peking kindergarten, a storage unit contained items to be used in the adjacent playground: jump ropes, balls, barbells, Ping-Pong and badminton equipment. Also on this shelf were small table blocks, dolls, animals, cars, and table games.

Materials used by the teachers for classroom lessons were observed in almost all rooms: accordions, tambourines, pianos or organs for accompaniment of singing and dancing exercises, paper cut-outs and flannelboard figures for arithmetic lessons, for example. As with many teaching materials, these were looked at and occasionally manipulated by the children but most often were used by the teachers and merely observed by the children. Large, colorful charts and posters would sometimes be hung on walls or be used on easels by the teachers.

During a meeting with several kindergarten teachers in Shanghai, we were told that during short periods of "free play" (before nine o'clock classes and during ten-minute breaks between classes), puzzles, books, and blocks were enjoyed by the children. We also were told at this meeting that water play (not observed during any session visited by our delegation) occurs during warm weather. It was explained that water is limited and its use controlled because it is not to be wasted. Frugality is universally a practical virtue in China.

Certain equipment standard in American nursery schools and kindergartens seemed to be missing—science materials (magnets, magnifiers, prisms, pulleys, plants, pets); table manipulanda (shapematching materials, lotto, dominoes, number rods); sets of unit blocks for floor constructions; dramatic play props (doll beds, small kitchen furniture, clothes for dressing up); large picture and story books; children's musical instruments, phonographs and records; children's easels and paints for large, free-form expressions and explorations. Sparsely furnished by American standards, the Chinese kindergartens seem to emphasize interactions among adults and children rather than the child's impact upon, and reaction to, things.

Outdoor play areas. Most of the outdoor kindergarten playgrounds we saw were well equipped, clean, and spacious, with low walls, shrubs, trees, walkways, benches, and a few flowers. Play yards were often an interior courtyard surrounded by buildings, and some of them could accommodate many groups of children at one time. There were, however, exceptions to this; sometimes the courtyard area could accommodate only one or two classes at a time and use had to be carefully scheduled. In a street kindergarten in Peking with an enrollment of nearly 200, for example, the courtyard area was only approximately forty feet square. Surfaces varied; some were of packed earth; others of cement or other hard material. Sometimes, in addition to or instead of the large playgrounds, there were small bare courtyards between rooms, which provided outdoor space for games, exercises, and large-muscle play.

On most playgrounds we saw substantial equipment: permanently positioned slides, swings, roundabouts, and basketball nets (about five feet off the ground). Some slides had three or four inclines, so that many children could descend at once in different directions. For the younger kindergartners, slides were designed to level off at the bottom. Many types of swing sets were observed. Some had the traditional single seat fastened to a frame with chain or rope; others had seats for as many as eight or ten children—in a single unit—a "boat" suspended in a large frame, for example. Several playgrounds provided small garden swings with bench seats facing each other, each with space for two riders.

Roundabouts were popular. Some seated children directly on the platforms; in other cases there were small metal chairs to sit in. A typical pattern of use for the roundabouts was for one group of children to sit in the chairs while an equal number walked around and pushed.

In addition, we saw children using portable equipment such as tricycles, jump ropes, hoops, rocking boats, Ping-Pong tables (with nets, without nets, and with blocks or bricks as substitution for nets), paddles and balls, badminton racquets and shuttlecocks. Materials like barbells, balls, and semaphore flags were used both in and out of doors. Some equipment was said to be made for the kindergartens by workers in nearby factories.

We were struck by the physical prowess of children. Young as they were, they were capable of extraordinary coordination and deft footwork as, for example, they skipped and danced in and out of elastic ropes (stretched by feet and legs of two "anchor men" standing about eight feet apart) or as, one by one, they practiced the skill of clenching a ball between their feet and then projecting it by a jump and thrust to see how far the ball could be cast forward. Ping-Pong balls and shuttlecocks flew through the air and seldom landed on the ground; boys with hoops practiced busily; teachers and children jumped rope together; a line of fifteen children charged through an obstacle course formed by slides, ropes, and climbers. Masses of children struggled cheerfully to win tug-of-war.

Not every playground featured all this activity, of course, but most of the playgrounds we were invited to see had all been well-furnished and were carefully maintained. Most important, they were supervised by teachers who involved themselves thoroughly with the children. Much outdoor activity was in the nature of musical games, tag, races, exercises involving adults and children in lively interchange.

There seemed to be an almost endless variety of relay races. Two teams would line up, with adults and children cheering and chanting, "chia-yu, chia-yu" (literally, "turn on the gas") at the sidelines. The cheer is directed toward all the racers; we did not see rooting for one team versus another, though we surely saw smiles of pleasure in victory. Then the children raced one at a time to the end of the course, perhaps a chair holding a teddy bear or a ball suspended on a rope, to be reached and struck, then back to his or her team. These races brought children and teachers alike to a high pitch of enthusiasm, which did not in our experience deteriorate into partisan wrangling or surging forward to have a turn.

Another game that elicited enormous energy and excitement was "three-deep tag," in which one player tries to tag another before the second scoots to one of the safety points in a circle of children. It was played in an open courtyard on one occasion during which several of us, unable merely to watch from the sidelines, joined in, to the surprise and pleasure of our Chinese hosts, kindergartners, and teachers.

Staff members from a large street-school kindergarten were asked whether they met together to coordinate their schedules; the answer was "Yes, but only for the use of the yard." We observed different groups of twenty or thirty children arriving in the courtyard in orderly lines headed by their teachers, playing for about half an hour and then moving back indoors. The small courtyard could easily have been overrun without such careful scheduling. On other playgrounds the size of a city block, the children appeared to stay within allocated zones and activities without moving to and through other groups; confusion was kept to a minimum.

These children at play seemed exuberant and controlled, with apparent sensitivity to their proper place in the order of things.

Wall displays. Upon entering an American kindergarten when the children are not there, one's attention is often initially engaged by children's art work, a seasonal poster or decoration made by the teachers, alphabet letters, colorful pictures of children at work and play, on the walls of the room. Not so in China. Many classrooms have no ornamentation at all apart from the ubiquitous portrait of Chairman Mao. In the East-is-Red Kindergarten there was a large, colorful collage on a main wall depicting children of the different national minorities of China. In some classrooms one would find a large blackboard decorated with colored chalk that conveyed some moral lesson. On an outside wall of most of the schools we usually met a blackboard decorated with a welcome to the American visitors.

The most common wall decoration other than the Chairman

Mao poster was one of several posters depicting scenes from the life of Lei Feng, who is clearly the chief folk hero of Chinese children nowadays. Selfless and dedicated to the principle "Serve the people," Lei Feng gave most of his spare time to helping his fellow soldiers and children. Lei Feng appears, in our short glance, to be a more readily assimilable model for little children than Mao Tse-tung, and he is immortalized in wall posters, periodicals, songs, and dances.

To an American visitor, more striking than the constant presence of Chairman Mao and the occasional presence of Lei Feng is the absence of art work done by the children, especially since art is one of the standard courses taught in kindergarten and is a talent the Chinese seem to treasure. Occasionally in primary schools we saw children's artwork on display, but always on special bulletin boards outside the classrooms. Not even on the walls of the art classroom would we find samples of the work of the children. In one primary classroom we found a table at the back of the room containing miscellaneous assortments of children's products, which we were free to take if we liked; on the walls, however, we found only the drawing by the instructor to be used as a model for that day's lesson.

We asked several groups of teachers about this absence of children's art, and almost always we received the answer that they did indeed display the children's productions. When we asked where, the reply was likely to be that they displayed it for festivals and special occasions. We saw none.

The curriculum

The curriculum in the Chinese kindergarten deals primarily with six subject areas: Chinese language and politics, mathematics, singing and dancing, drawing and painting, physical training, and productive labor. We shall discuss each of these areas in turn. A more analytic treatment of language learning will be given in chapter 7.

CHINESE LANGUAGE AND POLITICS. Language lessons for kindergartners were variously referred to as "politics" or "language"; besides beginning the formidable task of introducing children to a dialect not always like the child's usual speech (see chapter 7), "language lessons" served as means of moral and ideological indoctrination. Several summary themes emerged from our observations of language teaching in the kindergartens.

Language lessons as a framework for moral training. With one exception, every language lesson we observed carried a moral lesson and served to "raise the revolutionary consciousness" of the children. The procedures varied slightly, but the objectives never did. One teacher might point to pictures in a series of posters, and simply tell the children a story about the bitter past in which evil landlords oppressed the peasants. Another teacher might use the same posters but tell only part of the story and call on the children from time to time to relate other parts. Or a child might be asked to relate something he or she had done that exemplified the moral principle taught in the story. The stories presented in this manner almost always either directly carried a moral precept (give up your seat on the bus for an older person) or told about some act of heroism carried out by a child with whom the kindergarten children could identify.

One favorite story, which is also the subject of an animated cartoon and a ballet for adults, is called "The Cock Crows at Midnight." In this story a greedy landlord slips stealthily out to the chicken house in the middle of the night and pokes the cock with a stick so that the cock will crow and signal the peasants that it is time to go to the fields to begin work. The hero who discovers the treachery of the landlord is a small boy, thus perhaps facilitating identification on the part of the children. In the end the boy and the other peasants beat the landlord soundly for the way he has treated them. Another story repeated in several schools deals with a young girl whose grandfather is a skillful folk musician and is invited to Peking to play in a big theater. The little girl wants to go along but is persuaded of the importance of remaining behind in the countryside to work in the commune's vineyard. Later, by her efforts she increases the production of the commune and is taken by her grandfather to Peking. She takes a basket of grapes with her to give to Chairman Mao.

Acts of heroism, especially those involving children, apparently receive wide publicity in China. One frequently repeated story, which we also saw depicted in an animated movie and a ballet, is "Two Sisters on the Grassland," reported to be based on a real-life episode. It deals with two young sisters from a border province who are tending the sheep for their commune when a storm comes up. The sheep panic and run away. But the little girls, remembering that the sheep represent the economic life of their village, stay with them instead of returning to safety, and are lost in the blizzard. They are eventually found by their father and other villagers who have been searching for them, but not before the youngest girl loses a boot and has her foot frozen, forcing later amputation of some of the toes. Again, in reward, the sisters were personally received by Chairman Mao.

The moral is always drawn explicitly. After the children and the teacher have spelled out the lesson of the poster in detail, the usual question to the class is "Can you tell me who of the children in our class has followed Chairman Mao's thought?" or "Who in the class has done something that Lei Feng would do?" A four-year-old's response to the second question caused one of our hosts some anguish. She reported on one of her own good deeds, a response apparently so inappropriate that our host thought the teacher should be reprimanded for not correcting the child at once. To tell of one's own good deed is an act of selfishness; the child should have reported someone else's good deed.

Instructional materials to stimulate language learning. Most American kindergarten teachers would probably be surprised and dismayed at the prospect of having so few instructional materials to aid them in early teaching. Most striking is the almost total absence of books. In most primary and middle schools we were shown libraries, but not a single kindergarten had any large supply of books available. At story time we never saw a teacher reading a book to the children; rather, stories are told from posters or simply from the teacher's remembered store. Once in Canton and once in Peking we were ushered into a room in which the children were looking at books. We were told that children were given books to look at during their free play time, but as we were seldom in the schools at that period, we almost never saw any use of books.

Also apparently unavailable were any commercially produced materials (like the Peabody kits) to stimulate language development. Almost every classroom had a flannel board, but during our observations it was used more for mathematics than for language development. Puppets are very popular in China, but most of the other standard American props used to encourage language development—dramatic play materials, record players and tape recorders, lotto games, and so on—were seldom seen.

Group recitation. Chinese children memorize many poems, slogans, and stories that they recite in unison when called upon to do so. When we entered the Ta-an Lan-ying Kindergarten the three-year-olds stood up and recited what could only be considered an epic poem for children so young. Several of us remarked jokingly to each other that the length of the recitation exceeded physiological limits of memorization for such young children.

When teachers ask questions, cues are generally given as to whether all are to answer in unison or one child is to recite. If the former, all the children begin at precisely the same second and appear to follow exactly the same rhythm in the recitation. It should be noted that there is considerable security for the children in this kind of group recitation. If a child does not know the answer perfectly, he or she will not be embarrassed if the whole group is called upon to recite. And one can glance at another child for cues as to the expected answer when it is to be given in a group.

The group recitation not only involved collective answers to questions, but also the playing out of little dialogues. In such cases, it was always obvious that the children knew their lines in advance and that there was no improvisation in the exchange.

Conventional and rehearsed student responses are usual. With perhaps only a single exception, in Shanghai, every single language lesson we observed called for conventional and apparently rehearsed answers on the part of the children. "Who can tell what the girl (on the bus) should do?" Obviously the expected answer is that she should give up her seat. "What can one infer about the motives of the landlord from the picture?" Clearly, only some response such as, "He was greedy," would be acceptable. This, of course, fits into a schema in which language training must serve an ideological objective.

The Shanghai exception was notable enough to merit description. The lesson dealt with paper and its uses in society. The teacher sat down at the side of the desk with an array of different kinds of paper wrapped up in a white towel. Before she unwrapped her samples she asked the children to talk about paper and to tell her some of the things it was used for. We half expected the children to recite in unison a previously learned list of uses of paper. Here, however, children raised their hands and were called upon one by one. One child mentioned that paper was used for drawing; another mentioned wrapping packages; another said that it was used to make decorations for festivals. Clear evidence that the answers were spontaneous and not previously rehearsed came forth when one child mentioned that it was used in the toilet. Although perhaps a little embarrassed, the teacher accepted the answer and went immediately to the next child. After the children had exhausted their supply of spontaneous suggestions, the teacher unwrapped her supply of paper and then asked the use of each type. After each child's answer, the teacher would accept and then would elaborate on the response. Only once did she introduce a moral lesson, and that was when she held up a book. She commented on how much children enjoyed reading a book that was pretty and clean and had no torn pages and how sad it would be if the children failed to take care of the book and tore the paper. Significantly, she failed to add to her list of qualities of paper the fact that it tears easily.

We were told by administrators and teachers that since the

Cultural Revolution much greater emphasis had been given to democracy and discussion in classrooms. It is possible that this type of encouragement of divergent thinking, observed only once, actually occurs more frequently but was not shown to us. Perhaps the assumption was made that the group recitation mode is more impressive to foreign visitors. At any rate, well-rehearsed and uniform group response was unquestionably the predominant mode of participation we observed.

"Look and say" rather than "show and tell." Although the custom of having single children talk aloud and in a semiformal way to the group is frequently observed in the Chinese kindergarten, the pattern differs from the American style in at least one significant way. In American "show and tell" a child has some object to share with the other children and about which he talks when the group gets together. But instead of using concrete objects as support for verbal presentations, the Chinese teachers rely heavily on pictorial stimuli, and even label the instructional technique "look and say." The task for the child is to observe passively rather than act upon some kind of object, and then talk to his group. He does not describe things and their uses; rather, he tells moral stories based on pictures. Apparently the children take in significant amounts of information through this procedure of looking at pictures in classrooms (in perhaps the same passive way American children assimilate information from television), and they are expected to consolidate their knowledge verbally for their classmates.

In summary, language learning is a vital part of the kindergarten curriculum in China. It is highly formalized, places great stress on group recitation and memorization, and always serves as a vehicle for moral training.

Mathematics. Mathematics is regularly included in the kindergarten curriculum, with more time allotted to it for the older than for the younger children. It is easier for the Western visitor to follow mathematics instruction than to follow language instruction, since the Chinese use Arabic numerals. In the midst of the alien sounds and symbols, they greet the eye with a pleasant familiarity. Although we did not receive a detailed statement of the objectives for mathematics instruction from any educator, they appear to correspond very closely to the objectives for such instruction in American kindergartens. Children are familiarized with concepts of size and quantity, counting and enumeration, the concept of sets, one-to-one correspondence, and simple equations. Although we did not see any lessons in them, seriation and reciprocity may also be taught.

The mathematics instruction we observed, somewhat surprisingly, involved the children more than did language activities. For example, in a Sian kindergarten we observed a lesson for four-year-olds that required the recognition of numerals that named sets of certain quantities. The teacher had made some large, brightly colored, and attractive materials for the lesson. For example, there was one large radish on a card, two radishes, three radishes, and so on. Other cards had the numerals from one to nine written on them. She then set up two picture cards representing sets of different quantities on chairs in front of the room, and on another chair randomly laid out the numeral cards. She would call on two children to come forward and select from the chair containing the numerals those that corresponded to the sets that were pictured on the cards placed in the other two chairs. The children would run and quickly choose cards and then stand behind the chair containing the set described by the numeral they had selected. In general the children carried out the task with no errors, although on one occasion a child inverted the number as he held it up behind the set of objects. When this happened the children twittered excitedly but apparently not derisively, and the teacher smiled and suggested to the child that something was wrong.

In a Shanghai kindergarten we saw a mathematics lesson that dealt with simple addition operations. Using a variety of attractive props on the flannel board, the teacher carefully led the children through a series of operations involving: nine objects plus one object equals ten, eight objects plus two objects equals ten, on through five objects plus five objects equals a total of ten objects. After the children had counted with her as she placed objects on the flannel board, she took a series of preprinted cards containing the same equations without any objects to illustrate them—$9 + 1 = 10$, $8 + 2 = 10$, and so on. Throughout this lesson the children maintained a high level of interest in what the teacher was doing. She was an older teacher, and her skill in attracting and maintaining the children's attention and involvement in the task was most impressive.

Not surprisingly, the mathematics lessons also had a strong ideological flavor; in building examples, teachers preferred tractors to pets and canteens to flowers. One kindergarten number lesson started with an introduction about "your older brothers and sisters" who are serving the Revolution in the countryside.

SINGING AND DANCING. Of everything observed in Chinese kindergartens, nothing was more impressive than the skills shown by the children in their singing and dancing. In every school we visited, a high premium was placed on the acquisition of skills in singing and dancing. Most of the schools assign two class periods a week to this kind of activity, and in the selection of teachers some attention is always given to finding people who are skilled in this area and "enjoy singing and dancing with the children."

In almost every school we visited we were invited to observe a formal performance put on by the children, apparently a part of the program not only for visitors but also for parents and for special school celebrations. It usually took place in a special area of the school that had a stage or a relatively large unencumbered area and some kind of musical instrument. In one kindergarten in Shanghai, the piano was a seven foot grand—quite an unusual tool in kindergartens anywhere in the world! The performance almost always begins with a female child who comes forward and, in a very high-pitched voice, announces the first number, then does an abrupt about-face to the exit. All of the songs and dances presented by the children deal with ideological themes. In the one we named "The Big Apple," the lead child—we always saw girls in this role—comes forward and announces that she is monitor for the day and that she has the responsibility for distributing apples to her friends. With a charming melody in the background and with the chorus line performing an intricate dance step, she passes out apples to all but one of the children. Then she comes to the front of the stage and shares her dilemma with the audience. She now has only two apples left, one of which is large and one of which is small. Should she keep the big apple for herself and give the little one to her friend, or should she give the large one to her friend and keep the small one for herself? After thinking about Lei Feng and Chairman Mao, she realizes that the right thing to do is to keep the small one for herself. She cheerfully hands the big apple to her friend, and all the children then dance off the stage. Several times we saw this dance and song performed with real apples, but in one kindergarten cardboard props were used that exaggerated the difference between the size of the small apple and the big apple.

Apple Song

In the East-is-Red Kindergarten in Canton we saw a similar dance called "The Selfish Child." A new child comes to kindergarten and wants to play with all the toys instead of sharing with the other children. She picks up a lovely new metal airplane and claims it for herself. The other children soon teach her that Chairman Mao says to share, and eventually she gives up the plane and happily joins the other children in their play. Other songs and dances that we saw dealt with railway workers, peasants cutting grain in the fields, steelworkers producing steel for the state (and ending with a rather chilling call for all children of the world to unite in the revolutionary struggle), herdsmen tending flocks, truckers hauling produce for the peasants, and so on. Even the dances that represented the national minorities (Tibetans were favorites), or certain well-known folk customs, were accompanied by songs of ideological cast.

In the kindergarten in Shanghai we saw a long and elaborate dance that we labeled "The Ducklings," which resembled the kind of dances that young children in America might do—or at least they might do if taught. Two little girls are watching their ducklings and suddenly fall asleep. While they are asleep the ducklings run off, and the rest of the dance has to do with rounding them up and restoring the original situation. The children who played the ducklings engaged in more imaginative gestures and activities than we ordinarily saw. They shaped their mouths like duckbills and waddled around the room like little ducks. It was delightful and, again, remarkably well done.

The kindergarten music teacher supervises the performance, and plays whatever instrument is available. In addition to the announcer and the dancers, there is usually a chorus of from ten to twenty children who sit in chairs adjacent to the piano and take their cues from the musical director. Sometimes children in the chorus later get up and join in one of the dances, but more typically the dancers and the chorus will stay separate. We wondered whether the tendency to feature individual children in lead roles in the songs and dances was incompatible with the overriding cultural theme of selflessness and service to others. Upon inquiring about this at one kindergarten, we were told that several children could perform the lead roles and that indeed they did change off in these roles from one performance to another. Furthermore, the children were told that they were selected for the performances to do a service to their school, not to bring attention to themselves. The children who often had leads were also asked to undertake self-criticism to make sure that they were not taking the performance as an occasion for admiration of self.

The skill and expertise of the children in executing the songs and dances is phenomenal. They learn five, six, ten verses of the songs and perform complicated dances with grace and agility. The entire production is often done with a polish that approaches the professional. The major mysteries that remained after watching scores of performances by the young Chinese children are: How are such skills taught? By what patterns of splitting up the task, repeating the practice, rewarding the children, and so on are the abilities acquired? And to what degree are the dances and songs opportunities for expressing and resolving feelings and to what degree are they isolated "performances" in the narrower sense?

DRAWING AND PAINTING.   Drawing and painting are also considered important features of the Chinese kindergarten curriculum. Teachers are trained to instruct in these arts, and children are trained to acquire skill in them—to be in control of the materials and of certain formulae for presentation. Stencils are often used, and a teacher may present a model drawing in the front of the classroom for study and for copying—a task in which the children seem to excel. One may guess that the importance given tracing and precise reproduction in early drawing classes is, in part, a forecast of the way children will learn Chinese calligraphy, a demanding task to reach an aesthetic achievement.

During a discussion with kindergarten teachers in Canton, a group of four preschool children sat in our midst around a low table. They contentedly drew pictures while we talked together. We were interested not only in their air of quiet concentration while they drew but also in the competence of their work. They seemed not to experiment with line and design as American preschoolers might have; rather, they worked representationally with family figures, trees, houses, and flowers in clear, precise line drawings, many of which were apparently new copies of class exercises.

Although there were obviously some variations observed during our visit, the following description taken from the notes one of us took on an art class in the kindergarten run by a factory in Canton could perhaps be considered a prototype.

The task for the children was to color with pencils a trolley bus, the outlines of which had previously been duplicated and distributed to the children. On a display board at the front of the room the teacher had placed a previously colored model slightly larger than the one the children were to color. The children were seated on opposite sides of a long table, facing the teacher. On the table by each child were the picture of the trolley bus, and the colored pencils (yellow, blue, and black) he would need, lined up precisely at the back edge of the paper. Materials and children on both sides of the table were perfectly aligned. Each child's chair was placed at a right angle to the edge of the table, and each child faced the teacher and listened intently as she spoke.

After talking for a fairly long time about what the children were to do and how they were to color their pictures, the teacher took one of the duplicated designs, clipped it to the easel beside her, and began to color it as a model not only of structure but of procedure. Not a child touched pencils or design as the teacher colored her drawing and made suggestions about how the children were to proceed. When she finished, there were two models on the easel, the one previously prepared and on a slightly larger scale than the one to be completed by the children, and the exact model. Then, on a signal from the teacher, each child stood up, turned his chair around ninety degrees, picked up the yellow pencil and began to color that part of the trolley bus. The children worked very slowly and carefully. I drifted in and out of this classroom two or three times and found some of the children still carefully working on their drawings some twenty minutes later, with not a deviant color used and hardly a stroke out of place. The ones who had already finished sat patiently and waited for the others to finish.

Several of us visited a class in a Shanghai kindergarten of six- to six-and-a-half-year-old children who have two art classes per week for thirty minutes each. In this particular class, the children were asked by their teacher to draw a "thought picture." They had recently gone on a trip and were drawing their "thoughts" about the trip. Some drew structures, some animals or people, some flowers and trees. They used plain and colored pencils (and erasers) on pieces of eight-by-ten-inch paper. From the rather set formulae for tree–flower–sun–figure drawing, certain reflections of individual "thoughts" appear to emerge.

In these free-drawing sessions the children used no aids except small sticks to help them draw straight lines when needed. The children had obviously been taught certain skills that contributed to the maturity of their drawings. For example, when drawing trees (which generally looked like the poplars one sees all over China) they terminated the lines for trunk and branches when they got to foliage. Five- and six-year-old American children, unless taught otherwise, will typically permit all the branches to show through the leaves. Also, Chinese children use perspective, often using the centimeter stick to make the lines straight and enhance the effect. When we asked one teacher if she had shown the children how to draw lines to achieve perspective, her reply was that the children did it spontaneously. One of us then asked, "But what if the child does not spontaneously use perspective?" This time the answer was, "Then we would show him."

Another art lesson in a Shanghai kindergarten involved something else—a cooperative art project. In the class of four-and-a-half-year-olds we observed, the teacher had drawn a model on the blackboard, and each child was coloring six outlined balloons on a stenciled drawing of two children running with balloons. Older children in another room of this school had previously colored in the figures of the two running children; now the drawings were being passed down to these younger children for filling in the balloons! Presumably at the completion of the project there would be no quarreling over possession of the completed pictures. The teacher was instructing the children; "Use red and yellow crayons. Stay inside the lines." She told us in her gentle and easygoing manner that the children actually could use any colors they chose; on the pictures later given to us, however, all the balloons were indeed red and yellow.

We had taken with us to China many free-form paintings by American preschoolers. Our intention was to give them to Chinese kindergarten classrooms as signals of shared interests, and we did give away a few. After we had looked closely at the regular and radically different representational drawings of the Chinese children, however, we abandoned our plan, unwilling to explain to teachers that the multivariable abstracts we carried were "art" in young America.

Art techniques other than drawing and painting were also observed in various kindergartens: cutting and pasting, making collages, paper construction, and clay or plasticine modeling. Complicated plasticine figures modeled by kindergarten children were seen during two visits. In the first, children five and a half to six and a half were forming tiny tractors, horses with riders, bears, and people. Of course, some models were more competently turned out than others; but all the children worked intensely and managed to form astonishing shapes from the small bites of plasticine they assiduously pinched, rolled and formed. In another school, where children about five years old were eating lunch, some of their plasticine work was displayed on the window sills: miniature scenes of turtles, ducks in a pond, a boy pulling a wagon loaded with vegetables, a farm girl, a dog, and on and on. However one feels about representational modeling versus free exploration, there is no doubt that the children who made these figures had excellent control of their fingers.

PRODUCTIVE LABOR. Kindergarten teachers explained that love for manual labor is considered a virtue in Chinese society and that each kindergarten is called on to organize its own "factory." All the kindergarten children take part in some form of manual labor each week, typically for two twenty-minute periods. The periods are not considered demonstrations or exercises, but serious attempts to get children to experience manual labor and to produce useful products.

What do children accomplish? We saw a wide variety of kindergarten factories. Children tested flashlight bulbs, folded cartons in which the bulbs were to be packed for shipment, and inserted the bulbs into the forty or so holes in each carton. Children were given bowls of beans and taught to separate bad beans and stems from good beans. Under the supervision of adults, children planted and tended gardens. The children watered the plants with watering pails, pulled weeds, and gathered radishes and lettuce that were ready for harvest. At another school children assembled and organized materials for a sewing-machine factory. Some children tied plastic string onto labels and others opened and stacked small plastic envelopes into which screws or small parts could later be placed. All of these were activities in which the children could be successful and through which they could see that their efforts resulted in products that were useful to themselves or to other people. In one case, at least, the children were taken to see the factory where their own products were used.

Characteristics of the kindergarten classroom

Of necessity our description of the parts of the kindergarten curriculum has been brief, and all we could hope to do was present a thumbnail sketch of what is offered and what we saw in each class. But a few general characteristics of the entire program struck us as obvious.

IDEOLOGICAL SATURATION.   "We have been carrying out the revolution in education. Before the cultural revolution the children were shut up behind doors—they seldom went out but were kept inside the kindergarten. Now our policy is to run the school with doors open. That means the teachers will bring the children out to the factories and communes, and go out and do some physical labor such as collecting corn or gleaning the fields. Furthermore, the teachers will ask the children to tell stories about the past so they will not forget it and will be able to compare the past with the present."

The kindergarten curriculum is totally cohesive because of the ideological contribution that must be made by every activity in the daily routine. One does not encounter conflicts between such seemingly incompatible goals as wanting to encourage free expression and movement and wanting to train children to be quiet and attentive, to cite a conflict often identified in American kindergarten education. Every activity arranged for the child—and every activity is indeed arranged—must contribute to the child's "moral, intellectual, and physical" development in such a way as to prepare children "to carry the Revolution forward and move toward the ultimate goal of a classless society." Every activity must make the child want to serve the people.

Such cohesiveness should not shock American visitors with any sort of historical perspective, for, after all, we have created a vast public school apparatus to "prepare children for life in a democratic society." Anyone who has ever glanced at a McGuffey's *Reader* will remember that every exercise carried a moral lesson. And anyone who has observed the routine morning singing of "My Country, 'Tis of Thee" should not be surprised at the zest with which Chinese children sing patriotic songs and salute their flag. But we are accustomed in today's world to hear and see these declarations of support and then to hear and see something else—"The Wheels on the Bus Go Round, Round, Round," or nonsense like "The Eency-Beency Spider." What bumps American sensibilities hard in China is that the children almost never move beyond aphorism, even in songs and dances. Not even the "free art" can be said to escape, as many of the elaborately drawn pictures dealt with scenes in the lives of peasants or soldiers and were based on field trips designed precisely to stimulate such imagery. Thus the curriculum of the Chinese kindergarten apparently is designed to achieve virtually total solidarity with respect to national goals for young children. In one of the kindergartens we visited, the teachers held criticism and self-criticism sessions with their students once a week, to review and to evaluate their moral and academic progress.

HIGH STANDARDS OF SKILL ACQUISITION.   "We teach the children language so that they can express themselves better; arithmetic so that they can count, add, and subtract; music, so that they can sing; fine arts so they can draw and play with clay; and physical training so they can become strong and healthy."

This brief quotation exemplifies the strong emphasis in all areas of the curriculum on the acquisition of skills and competencies. Nowhere is there any evidence of inclusion of an activity in the program simply for its own sake. In each subject area the standards are high. Children are taught by example and positive suggestion, as the teachers are said to consider individual criticism and punishment to be undesirable modes of improving performance. Children are taught to speak loudly and clearly, and an inadequate response is elaborated by the teacher. As the children draw or use clay, the teacher circulates through the room providing suggestions for improvement or additions that might be made. A child who responds incorrectly in an arithmetic game is asked to observe the other children and try again.

Nowhere are the high standards more apparent than in the children's theatrical performances. For half an hour or more the children perform a series of dances, songs, and skits in which there rarely if ever is a missed cue, an awkward step, or a forgotten song. The level of skill is remarkable, as is the confidence with which the children present themselves on stage. Generally, the impression one gets from observing the children in all their activities is that the high standards are not a source of anxiety but of controlled satisfaction.

STRUCTUREDNESS OF THE DAILY PROGRAM. The following daily program for one boarding kindergarten was posted in the courtyard:

6:30– 7:00	Get up
7:00– 7:30	Wash and exercise
7:30– 8:00	Eat
8:00– 8:40	Free activity
8:40– 9:00	Class
9:00–10:30	Free play, marching, wash hands, prepare to eat

10:30–11:00	Lunch
11:00–11:30	Prepare for nap
11:30– 2:30	Rest
2:30– 3:30	Get up, wash, snack
3:30– 3:50	Class
3:50– 5:00	Free activity, marching, wash hands, prepare to eat
5:00– 5:30	Dinner
5:30– 7:00	Free activities
7:00– 8:30	Eat snack, wash hands, face, and body
8:30	Bed

Most of the kindergartens we visited followed a program in which the time was as tightly structured as in this example or even more so, although, as we have emphasized, few of China's kindergartens board children. In outdoor play the children moved, as a group, from one activity to another, so that the whole school appeared to follow a carefully orchestrated pattern. As the last child in one group reached the bottom of the slide, another group was at the slide area and the first of the group was ready to climb the ladder. When outdoor play space is limited, as it often was in urban kindergartens, or when equipment is limited, as it was in most of the kindergartens, this degree of efficiency in use of space and materials would seem to be necessary. What individual play there was (and we are sure we would have seen more on a longer visit) took second place to the activities of the group.

The indoor play we saw was also highly organized. Unstructured play in the Chinese kindergarten (with American visitors present) seemed not to imply that the child is free to pursue his choice among activities. Rather, in our circumscribed observation, it meant that within an assigned activity, the child might play freely. The children were seated at their desks or tables and given boxes of colored pencils and sheets of paper; they were then free to draw whatever they wish. Or they were given colored plasticine, small blocks, scissors and colored paper, or squeeze toys and dolls, the group typically being supplied with the same materials at the same time. Free play often involved friction or windup toys. Because there were so few toys, the teacher would often wind up the toys and have the children simply watch as the chicken laid its eggs, the Ping-Pong game began, or the siren of the fire truck whirred. Everything we saw was on cue, and no one except the children of foreign diplomats missed a cue.

WHAT IS NOT IN THE PROGRAM.   From the point of view of preschool practice in the United States and other Western countries, there are a number of striking omissions from the Chinese kindergartens we saw. Perhaps the most obvious is the apparent limitation of choice. The child did not decide what he would do; nor did he move about the room from one activity to another. As in an earlier era in American education, every activity seemed to have its time and place, and all the children followed the fixed schedule. Indeed, except for one kindergarten in Peking, all children in a class did the same thing at the same time.

A second conspicuous omission is the virtual absence of problem-solving tasks as standard classroom activities. At least in the preschool years, we seldom saw the child presented with any activities that required him to figure out what to do or to consider alternative solutions. When this point was pressed in an interview with several kindergarten teachers they spoke of giving puzzles to the children; and we were able to purchase some jigsaw puzzles in a toy store, but we saw such materials in use in only one classroom. Uniformly, children were being taught skills for performing preset tasks rather than strategies for approaching new problems.

Perhaps most striking of all, given the great emphasis in Chinese educational ideology on collectivism and working together, was the rare occurrence of cooperative activities. There were rarely, if ever, group projects or opportunities for teamwork at the preschool level. Productive labor in the situations we observed invariably took the form of a solitary task, each child folding his own paper boxes, sorting beans, and so on. One of the rare instances of antisocial behavior we saw (at the July First Commune in Shanghai) involved a three-year-old, who, in sorting out defective beans from a pile, surreptitiously slipped a few into the already sorted pile of his neighbor.

In contrast to the ever-present and typically brilliant songs, dances, and theatrical performances, we rarely observed any spontaneous dramatic play—no playing house or doctor's office, so common in preschool settings elsewhere around the world. The dramatic play we observed (people on a train helping an old lady home from work, storekeeping, feeding dolls) all apparently followed a previously written scenario.

Note should be taken of the absence of negative behavior toward the children on the part of the staff. We seldom observed disapproving gestures and acts of even mild punishment appeared to be genuinely rare. Of course, within the framework of the teachers' objectives for the children, we never saw any child behavior likely to elicit a negative response. Teachers and staff members established an atmosphere of warmth, approval, and perhaps most important, the confident expectation that each child would behave himself appropriately and succeed in the task at hand.

The teachers and caregivers

"We love our work because the children are the future generation. They are the successors of the revolutionary cause. We are proud to dedicate our time to this work. Our work in the past was divorced from practice. Therefore we failed to carry out faithfully Chairman Mao's revolutionary line. That is why a lot of changes in early childhood education have been made since the Cultural Revolution."

One does not achieve the high level of similarity among kindergartens we saw and among educational philosophies expressed by teachers we visited without an effective communication network reaching all the adults likely to be involved in designing and executing kindergarten programs. How have teachers been trained so that the daily program, or at least talk about the daily program, emerges uniformly in each school? Knowing something about the educational upheavals that accompanied the Cultural Revolution, we were eager to know how the "rectification" programs affected kindergarten teachers and what changes had been made in teacher training since the Cultural Revolution.

TRAINING BEFORE AND AFTER THE CULTURAL REVOLUTION. Even though the present Chinese kindergarten curriculum was formulated before the Cultural Revolution, it "had not been carried out to the full," according to Peking educational officials with whom we spoke. Teachers were said to have been content to care for the children and to play with them. But since the Cultural Revolution, the ideology of Chairman Mao has apparently been taught systematically to kindergarten children by teachers who have been trained in effective ways of presenting it. An example that we saw frequently is the look-and-say exercise in which class struggle and Maoist thought are presented on posters and charts in class, with the teachers eliciting conclusions and responses from the children.

Many kindergarten teachers (the proportion is not clear) have graduated from middle school. Some have gone on to take three years of special training in art, piano, dance, physical culture, language, mathematics, science or "common knowledge," and teaching methods. In the East-is-Red Kindergarten in Canton, most of the teachers are normal-school graduates. But in many Chinese cities, normal schools closed down at the beginning of the Cultural Revolution; in some instances, they are only now beginning to operate again. And the number of Chinese kindergartens has increased so rapidly that now, apparently, there are not nearly enough college-trained personnel. As a result, and for ideological reasons as well, teachers are recruited from the ranks of factory or farm workers or from educated youth; some are prepared in special training classes of from three to six months' duration, but most are trained in work–study programs. Of sixty staff members in the Cotton Mill Kindergarten in Peking (#3), we were told that two had graduated from normal school and ten had attended short courses; the rest had presumably received only in-service training.

We learned during discussions with kindergarten teachers that they often meet not only to discuss political thought but to exchange and extend experience and techniques—within their own schools and also at times with teachers from other schools. Within any one kindergarten, the Revolutionary Committee members of the school administration are reported to meet frequently with teachers and to ask them to "check the education program and the health of the children." In both day and boarding kindergartens teachers sew new costumes, play various musical instruments, and assume responsibility for general health care and the teaching of hygiene, even caring for children suffering minor illnesses if need be.

Work–study training is the prevalent pattern in China. At one kindergarten, we were informed that beginning teachers receive an informal orientation during which they observe experienced teachers, and then gradually join in; they work under the guidance of the longtime teachers and are able to learn by discussion and exchange. The old Communist theme of teachers as "open to criticism" has apparently received new emphasis since the Cultural Revolution; teachers report that criticism is a way of improving and understanding their work; they have learned, too, to take direction in part from the Revolutionary Committee members and from parents as well as from educational specialists. When we pressed for specific examples of parent participation, however, we were told much more often about teachers' advice to parents than parents' criticism of teachers.

TEACHING SCHEDULE. The work week in China is six days for everyone and teaching schedules are based on a six-day week. Teachers generally work eight-hour days, we were told; in some kindergartens, however, they work on overlapping shifts to accommodate varying needs of families. Also, some teachers work split shifts, with time out at midday. Kindergartens for day care generally operate from about seven in the morning until six or seven in the evening, with children, teachers, and "nurses" or care-givers fitting into various time schedules according to their specific needs. During childrens' naps, teachers may be free for dis-cussions and study. In one kindergarten, teachers are freed to pre-pare materials and the next week's lesson twice each week, with one half day each week free to devote to professional study and two hours every week given over to political study. Kindergarten teachers in Shanghai described working days as follows: every class has two teachers; one teaches the children in the morning, and the other takes over in the afternoon. Each teacher has one-half day each week for classroom preparation and study. In ad-dition to scheduled classes and playground supervision, some teachers help with rehearsals for children's performances; skits and songs may take from two to four weeks of afternoon rehearsal so that those adults involved are scheduled accordingly. Teachers are said to be granted one month vacation every year. We were informed that they generally take two weeks of vacation during the summer and the other two weeks during the winter months, apparently at times when the schools are closed. Children's activi-ties are supervised even during school vacations, and some teach-ers may participate in such supervision.

According to the figures we were given (not always easy to assess accurately because of problems in translation and the wide variation in ways of designating staff) most kindergartens in China maintain a staff ratio of children to all adults of about nine to one; the ratio of children to teachers is approximately fifteen to one. Because many "staff members" are actually assistant teachers in training, however, the nine-to-one ratio is the more useful figure for comprehending the reality of the personal and involved teach-ing we observed.

WARMTH AND AFFECT. Within the limitations on making judgments about affect in another culture, we felt that Chinese teachers were uniformly gentle, soft-spoken, and warm in their tone and manner, although there was not a lot of touching or hug-ging between teachers and children. Since we saw few instances of distress or crying, there was little opportunity to see how responsive the teachers might be or how quickly they would react to children in distress. Our impression and our occasional observation was that teachers responded quickly and efficiently to these situations. The fact that the children seldom needed comforting intersects then with the prevailing cultural pattern of rewarding children with verbal praise rather than touching or hugging. In a sense, the devoted support and affection Chinese adults give to children is, at once, more reliable, more general, and less intimate than we are used to seeing among Americans.

CONTROL TECHNIQUES. The general absence of aggression, shoving, pushing, grabbing of property, and rough-and-tumble play among Chinese kindergartners meant that there were few opportunities to witness the teachers' preferred control techniques. When such teacher interventions did occur, they were likely to involve gentle, physical removal of the child from the setting, sometimes with a quiet accompanying remark. Teachers had no difficulty talking about what they did when a child was "naughty." "We persuade him" was always the reply. Apparently their gentle persuasion is very effective.

When the child performed a task with competence, mild but not unusually enthusiastic praise was given; a nod and a quiet remark were the typical reaction. It appears that the stated public philosophy of socialization is in accord with the teachers' actual practices, at least in our presence and in the schools we visited. The teachers, like the children, were, again to our culturally unskilled eyes, relatively homogeneous in their behavior across settings, and although there was clear variation in competence, the teachers we saw impressed us with their devotion to young children and to their teaching tasks.

The children

As we went from school to school in China, we constantly asked one another, "How can children accept all this regulation and control, and away from the family at that?" In short, we looked for

possible costs of the teaching procedures as well as for gains, for
clues as to what compromises with ordinary developmental routines are being made. Chinese kindergartners, like healthy young
children everywhere, are attractive, and their ability to charm
visitors with their songs and dances has already been described.
But what other characteristics could be noted in a somewhat
superficial visit such as we had?

AFFECT AND SOCIABILITY.   The kindergarten children could
shift easily and quickly from a posture characterized by motor and vocal quiescence and focused attention to one of effer-
vescence and gaiety in a few seconds. A good example of their
ease of transition occurred when one of us taught "London
Bridge" to a group of Sian kindergarten children. The children
enjoyed the novelty of the new song and movements and laughed
and smiled continually. One girl, for example, laughed excitedly
for the entire twenty minutes the dance was being taught. This
observation may be important, for it is sometimes assumed that
docility and conformity do not go along with the capacity for
spontaneous laughing, smiling, and motor excitement. Chinese
children provide a striking disconfirmation of any such hypothesis.
    Additionally, the children seemed bold and minimally timid
with us. They approached, took our hands, examined our cameras,
sang solos, and danced without apprehension. Rarely did we see
signs of anxiety or fear, and crying and whining were virtually absent. There were no instances of rage, anger, or temper tantrums.
We were told that some children in boarding kindergartens are
homesick for a few weeks if they have not lived in a collective
context before, but the teachers quickly added that within one or
two weeks the children gained control and adjusted to the new
living arrangement. Teachers told such children that being willing
to let the parents go was the child's "contribution to the social
welfare."
    Positive affect and sociability are thus common, while visible
signs of fear, anxiety, and anger are rare. Some of us felt that the
kindergarten years may be the "best years" for the contemporary

Chinese child; he is too young to engage in heavy physical labor and the demands of primary school but old enough to understand what is asked of him and competent enough to meet those requests.

CONCENTRATION AND SELF-CONTROL.   One of the most impressive qualities of the Chinese kindergarten children we saw was their ability to sit calmly for long periods of time—waiting for a turn to play with a ball, waiting for a turn to sing, listening to a story told by a teacher or classmate, or just being a spectator. They do not nervously poke their neighbors, shuffle their feet, pick at their faces, or shift their trunks. On one occasion, thirteen of us entered a room in which a large number of kindergarten children had just awakened from their nap. Hardly looking at us the group rose from their beds, efficiently folded their bedding, took their blankets to the side of the room, dressed themselves, and walked out, with no shyness, giggling, or distraction from their mission. On a second occasion, we saw thirty-five six-year-olds quietly cutting paper; none was distracted by the thirteen of us walking into the room and all remained oriented toward the task.

The Chinese children we saw seemed to have an ability to attend with laserlike focus to what adults were saying to them. As we have already noted, they can memorize lengthy songs and long passages of dramatic lines that some American teachers regard as too difficult for nursery-school children. In a boarding kindergarten in Sian, the music teacher taught a group of six-year-olds a new song in only ten minutes, with about a half a dozen repetitions by the teacher and the class. In Shanghai, we saw a kindergarten child give a three-minute recitation about Norman Bethune and three five-year-olds put on a ten-minute skit without a flaw. All the children knew their lines well and the performance was remarkably well coordinated. In a commune outside Shanghai we saw a group of six-year-olds sit for almost half an hour separating good and bad pea beans into separate bowls. In other places we saw kindergarten children painstakingly copying a blackboard drawing of a man, waiting patiently to be selected for a dance game, standing quietly by the wall of a building without moving or shoving. In classrooms, the children sit with hands still and feet planted on the floor.

It is not possible to list all the factors that might contribute to the striking self-control of Chinese children. The experience of being bundled up in unheated nurseries might be one determinant. But since the child in tropical Canton also shows this trait, that explanation loses power. Teachers and probably parents consistently restrain restless motor activity as soon as it appears. We observed one episode in Shanghai where the teacher allowed some five-year-olds to play freely with a ball. In a few minutes the play had become slightly unordered. The teacher immediately stepped in and initiated a structured game. It is possible that consistent discouragement of restless or unstructured activity has produced the quiescence the Chinese child displays. This explanation gains strength from the fact that children in the rural areas were generally more restless and distractable than the children in the more structured, urban kindergartens we visited.

Yet this speculation about early external structuring is not sufficient. Merely discouraging restlessness would not lead automatically to the ability to focus and to listen carefully to what adults are saying. We can be relatively confident only about the facts of control and concentration in the children, the high degree of structure in the kindergarten routines, and the clear centrality of the adults as initiators, maintainers, and terminators of all activities. There is little support for babyishness and dependent behavior; the Chinese child seems expected to keep his emotions as well as his activity under control.

ANTISOCIAL BEHAVIOR. During our three weeks in China we saw thousands of young children, in schools, in their neighborhoods, in parks, and on city streets. Almost never did we see any antisocial behavior. Although it would be easy to say that we were not observing typical situations, this interpretation does not seem to us to be valid. Some of us lingered in kindergarten rooms after the main party had left, or returned to groups or activities alone.

We went to parks and walked city streets alone, and only once did we observe a clearly aggressive act on the part of a child and almost never did we observe a teacher behave in an obviously harsh way toward a child.

An incident of aggressive behavior we did observe took place in a kindergarten during outdoor play. One boy shoved another to the ground; the second boy cried. Quickly the teacher came over, sent the aggressor off, and comforted the crying child. In a moment the aggressor returned, apparently on the cue of another teacher, and helped brush the dust off the victim's clothes. We would have expected a higher incidence of such incidents in kindergartens, where the children were together in groups of twenty to thirty children for long hours, and where there was by conventional American standards a shortage of materials or toys. The low incidence of antisocial behavior may be ascribable in part to the highly structured environments in which the children lived. More important, however, it seemed to us that the teachers were unusually alert and involved, and did not leave the children on their own for any length of time or with any great frequency.

Important also may be the general philosophy that is said to guide the kindergarten movement in China, which teachers expressed in similar ways: "We teach the children Chairman Mao's thought. Chairman Mao teaches us to care for each other, to love each other. If a child hits another child we will talk to them, and find out who is right and who is wrong. We get them to have self-criticism. We hope to teach the children to care for each other, so they will get the spirit of serving the people when they are very small." The goal of kindergarten education in China, as explained by one teacher, is "to prepare the children for primary school and so they will grow into workers with socialist consciousness and become successors to the revolutionary cause." With the skepticism of American intellectuals, we tended to view such statements largely as empty ritual, but insofar as the ideas animate and direct teachers, it is not surprising that consistently prosocial behavior is highly prized in China, and that antisocial behavior is seen as a violation of the goals of the whole kindergarten effort.

But what happens when the child does show aggression, say by taking a toy from another member of the group? In answer to this question, one teacher responded, "We play with toys in a group. For example, we have lots of kitchen toys. We give these to a group of children. One will be a cook, one will be an assistant. The children learn from workers. The children play bus. Someone will be the driver, someone the conductor, others are passengers. Each has his own part."

Perhaps as impressive as the lack of antisocial behavior was the lack of traditional western marks of tension. None of us observed sustained thumb-sucking, nail-biting, tics, masturbation, or other tension-reducing behaviors in kindergarten children. Why we did not observe any examples of this type of behavior is not clear; there may be culturally defined signs of the cost of high structure that were invisible to us or there may be later effects—perhaps in patterns of problem-solving or in creativity—that only longer, closer study will reveal. But one conclusion is clear: the careful control exerted on interpersonal aggression is not accompanied by any signs of tension or anxiety that experienced Western observers can readily detect.

SEX DIFFERENCES.   Sex differences were more salient in the differential actions of teachers than in the spontaneous behavior of children. As in the case of the younger nursery children, the infrequency of aggression put one sex difference to which we were accustomed out of sight. Further, since few of the children were overtly dependent or fearful, sex differences were minimal there. However, teachers reported that boys were more aggressive than girls, although no sex difference in dependency or fear was reported.

Many teachers spontaneously separated the sexes in seating arrangements in classrooms and outside. In a kindergarten attached to a textile factory in Sian, we saw six separate groups of children arranged in sex-segregated groups. On one occasion we saw trios of children participate in a race and the teacher carefully avoided mixing the sexes in these trios. In many organized settings sex segregation was the rule, although there were exceptions. The most striking sex difference we saw occurred for singing and dancing. The majority of the performances involved more girls than boys. The teachers remarked that girls seemed to like this activity more than boys and seemed to be more competent in it. Again, the sources of the variation are unknown to us.

PHYSICAL HEALTH.   Medical services were available to all of the kindergartens we visited. Large schools with several hundred children sometimes maintained their own medical services; the Kindergarten #5 in Peking, where 255 children were said to be boarding, had a clinic with doctor and nurse. In a more modest street kindergarten in the same city, one of thirty staff members had special medical knowledge and training gained from a course she had taken in a district hospital.

Children with minor illnesses stay in their kindergartens and are cared for by the staff. Kindergarten staff members appear quite knowledgeable in matters of hygiene, physical training, nutrition, and health care. Sometimes there were isolation areas for mildly sick children. For more serious illnesses, children are apparently taken to a clinic or hospital by their parents or, if need be, by a teacher or health worker.

A fuller description of health care is presented in chapter 8 of this report. We believe Chinese kindergarten children are generally healthy, strong, and full of zest.

A word in summary

Against the backdrop of American preschool education, with all its diversity and variation, several characteristics of Chinese kindergartens warrant emphasis.

The daily program of the Chinese kindergarten is regular, tightly scheduled, structured, centered on adults, with lessons carefully dosed to the young child's attention, concerned with language skills and arithmetic, and heavily emphasizing politics, dancing, singing, and drawing. The children seem expressive, docile, controlled, of concentrated attention, remarkably skillful in dancing and the arts, nonaggressive, compliant, unfearful, and without obvious symptoms of anxiety or tension.

When we tried to discern what characteristics of teaching procedure or tactics were potentially relevant to the development of children like these, we could come up only with a list for further investigation. Prominent on the list, and noteworthy for most of us, were the high ratio of approval by teachers to disapproval, the reliance on teaching by repetition and by formula, the repeated use of models from the past and present, the use of persuasion and moralistic reasoning (even with the very young), the close connection between words about teaching and teaching practice, and, perhaps above all, the almost serene certainty of the teachers that the children would, of course, do as they were taught. In turn, the children learn to expect that they can acquire the skills and the personality traits that the teachers expect them to acquire. We do not know the relative importance of these characteristics, nor do we understand how they interact with one another or how they are applied to bring forth desired behavior on the children's part.

As we begin our consideration of children in primary schools, we will keep in mind the traits observed already in kindergartners and the questions already raised by our observations of them.

Morning calisthenics in a primary school. To brisk marching music, a student leads hundreds of his schoolmates in routine daily exercises.

Row monitors in a primary school carry out morning inspection, to determine whether or not everyone has a clean face, clean hands, a handkerchief, and a cup. Length and neatness of hair are also sometimes evaluated.

Seated by twos (in primary school, oftentimes a boy and a girl share a desk), students raise their hands to be called on. When a name is called, the child will stand straight at the side of his desk and call out the answer.

5. PRIMARY SCHOOLS

Lesson One
Quotations from Chairman Mao

You should concern yourselves with affairs of state and carry through the Great Proletarian Cultural Revolution to the end.

—First lesson in English for primary students

Because our Chinese hosts were unprepared for our interest in schooling beyond kindergarten, we had far fewer opportunities to observe school-age children than we wished for. To our previous caveats about the slim base of our data must therefore be added even further reservations about our descriptions of the primary and middle schools. In particular, we want to call attention to two significant ways in which our sample of three primary schools was unrepresentative of primary schools in China more generally. First, they were all old; as we note later, they were built before 1949 and all of them can probably make claim to a certain tradition and experience in primary school education. Second, and perhaps of greater consequence, they were all urban. The glimpse we had of primary schools in the country, as well as the testimony of our hosts, suggests that rural schools are likely to be less well endowed in physical plant, less able to draw on specially trained teachers, and not so well equipped for after-school activities. We also suspect, though we cannot provide observations in support of our belief, that rural schools may be more closely geared than those we saw to training students for the practical tasks of agricultural production. Finally, rural schools must adapt their schedules to the demands of planting and harvesting.

We were told that in most areas children enter primary school

115

at age seven, but there are exceptions; in Shanghai for example, and perhaps elsewhere as well, the entering age is six and a half. The number of years in primary school also varies. Some schools are still on the six-year primary system that Mao Tse-tung criticized during the Cultural Revolution. One school we visited in Peking was graduating its last sixth-grade class in 1974; for the younger children, the curriculum has been reorganized in the attempt to teach in five years the material that was previously covered in six, and children will be sent on to middle school after five years of primary. Shanghai is also said to be in transition, still teaching six years throughout its primary school system. The age of leaving primary school probably varies from twelve to fourteen.

Some schools are on half-day shifts for the youngest primary children. Shanghai is said to have a shortage of buildings and teachers for the primary schools; in some areas of the city, children in the first three grades attend only in the morning or the afternoon but not both. We do not know how widespread this situation is elsewhere in China.

By and large children seem to attend schools in their own neighborhoods. We were told that the practice represents a change from the old days, where there were fewer schools, fees were high, and particular schools catered to certain kinds of families, with the result that children often either traveled a considerable distance to school or boarded. There are still a few primary schools where children may board, but the vast majority are apparently neighborhood-based day schools.

The three primary schools we visited had all been built prior to the Revolution, and all of them were formerly British-style private schools. The more recently organized schools may have physical plants that are more crowded and less suited to the educational tasks of a school. The primary school we saw usually had several two-story rectangular and barrackslike structures oriented around one or more courtyards. The courtyards were either paved or of hard-packed dirt, and there were few trees or shrubs. There were basketball hoops, but little other stationary equipment. The buildings we saw were of grey brick or stone, unadorned. Classrooms on the ground floor usually opened directly onto a courtyard, without indoor corridors. In Peking, most classrooms received some heat from small stoves or radiators; in Sian and Shanghai, the rooms were unheated and the windows were open. During our days in Sian, the temperature in the classrooms was seldom over fifty degrees in the morning. Our breath was visible; the children shivered and rubbed their hands, and a few wore cloth gloves.

Classroom furnishings were almost invariably spartan—rows of flat double desks, wooden benches, and a plain wooden table at the front of the room for the teacher. Usually, at each double desk there was one boy and one girl; the usual overrepresentation of boys forces an occasional boy–boy pairing, but girl–girl pairings were less common and in two of the schools rare indeed. Except in science classes, equipment was limited to a large blackboard on the front wall, surmounted by a picture of Chairman Mao. In one classroom there was a large pull-down map of China. There were virtually no pictures or other decorations on the walls, save the ever-present picture of Chairman Mao and an occasional instructional poster—for example, a representation of eye exercises. Again, there was some variation; in one Peking third grade, we even saw awards posted on the wall (a class prize for excellence in jump rope and what were said to be individual awards as well).

Pupils typically worked from individual pamphlet-style books. They had small notebooks and pencil boxes. They wrote with ballpoint pens, with pen and ink, and sometimes with pencils.

Class size and teacher load

The primary school in Peking was said to have 1,150 students, divided into twenty-eight classes; the one in Shanghai, 1,800 students in thirty-four classes; class size is commonly fifty to fifty-five students. A class remains in its "homeroom" for nearly all its classroom work, while teachers move from classroom to classroom, teaching their specialized subjects. Each class, however, has a homeroom or responsible teacher who does most of the home visiting and other communcation with parents for a given class of students. There are apparently more teachers than classrooms. The Peking school was reported to have seventy-one teachers and staff members for twenty-eight classes, Shanghai had seventy-five for thirty-four classes. In the Sian primary school, the teaching staff was smaller in relation to the number of classes. Teachers commonly teach about fifteen class hours a week. During their hours out of class, the teachers are engaged in class preparation, teachers' meetings (including twice-weekly political training meetings), meetings with groups of student representatives, supervision of workshops, grading workbooks, and home visits. The teacher's day runs from seven-thirty to five, six days a week; individual teachers sometimes remain at school after five. Home visits apparently are often made during the evening hours. A few unmarried teachers live on the school grounds (probably a rare arrangement) and are available to help supervise children whose parents, perhaps on evening work shifts, are not at home by five. We do not know how often children stay in school into the evening hours.

Urban schools are on holiday for approximately four weeks in winter and five weeks in midsummer, but the teachers do not have this entire time off. A staff of teachers remains at the school throughout vacation periods to help supervise extracurricular activities; and part of the time is used in teacher-supervised trips to factories, parks, and exhibits.

Objectives of primary education

The principals of the three primary schools we visited at some length, although working in three different provinces, presumably with a considerable degree of administrative decentralization, articulated remarkably uniform educational goals in their briefings about their schools. The general objectives were the same as those we have described for kindergarten education. The changes that the Cultural Revolution had brought about were stressed, including increased emphasis on political training, participation in school administration by workers and peasants, student participation in and respect for productive labor, teaching "practical" rather than merely theoretical knowledge, physical fitness, and the preventive aspects of health care. The student, we were told, had to be made to understand that the purpose of their education is not to further their own careers and to make them members of an intellectual elite; rather, it is to enable them to serve the people.

The schedule of a school day

The basic pattern of the day reported for the three schools we observed closely involved three class periods of forty minutes each in the morning, with a thirty minute break between the second and third periods. The first portion of the break is spent in two standardized activities—a set of eye exercises believed to strengthen eye muscles and prevent nearsightedness (posters illustrating the exercises appeared occasionally on classroom walls) and a set of calisthenic exercises done en masse to recorded music. The lunch break is from eleven-thirty to one-thirty, and most students go home. In the afternoon there are two class periods followed by optional after-school activities.

Children arrive at school neatly dressed in clothing that is varied and colorful compared with the clothes of adults or even of middle-school students. The number of layers varies with the weather; we were told six layers are usual when it is quite cold and children keep on their outer garments in the classroom. The boys' hair is worn in crew cuts or shorter; the girls wear their hair in pageboys or in short braided pigtails.

The opening events of the day vary from school to school. In the school in Peking, the children placed their handkerchiefs and their metal drinking cups on their desks. Row monitors then moved down the rows of desks, making sure each child had a clean handkerchief and cup, and inspecting each child's neck, hands, and fingernails. The monitors reported to the teacher, who congratulated the class on the fact that only one child had forgotten to bring his cup and that everyone had passed handkerchief and neck and hand inspection. In the primary school in Sian, where we were also present at the beginning of the day, there was no such inspection.

In Peking, classes began at eight, and the children were asked to be at school ten minutes ahead of the bell. In this school of 1,150 pupils, we saw no child arriving late. The principal, when asked what was done if a child was tardy, replied simply, "No one is." When pressed, he said that in the rare instances where a child's parents had not gotten the child up on time, the teacher talked with the child and, if necessary, with the parents; there was usually no further problem.

In a school in another city, by contrast, approximately thirty children arrived running at the school entrance after the bell had stopped ringing. Tardiness was recorded in each classroom, and the classroom record was posted on the bulletin board, with awards given to the classes with the best records. Individual children who were tardy several times were reportedly talked to by the teacher and by the Little Red Soldiers.

The curriculum

The subjects taught in the schools we saw were Chinese language, arithmetic, political thought, music, art (including calligraphy), common knowledge (elementary science, geography, and history), and physical education. We understood that military training began in the fifth and sixth grades, and that both drill practice and training in rifle use are included, but we never observed military training. We did see pictures of it in a display case in a primary school where the various activities of school children were depicted.

In a separate section of the report (chapter 7) the teaching of reading is discussed. Here we will first describe the way several classes we observed were conducted and then attempt some generalizations about teaching methods.

A LESSON IN ARITHMETIC: FOURTH LEVEL (AGE TEN). The lesson has to do with computing the surface areas of a box. A box is held up and the teacher points out that it has three pairs of surfaces. She gives the dimensions of the box ($3 \times 7 \times 9$ cm.) and asks for the area of the top surface. The children shout out the answer. Then she points out that the bottom surface has the same dimensions, so its area is the same. The teacher writes on the board *$9 \times 7 = 63, 63 \times 2 =$* , then calls on a child, who rises and gives the answer, which the teacher writes on the board. Two others are called on to supply the areas of the two other pairs of surfaces. The teacher then asks for the total surface area. There is a pause while the children mentally add the three numbers— they do not use scratch paper for this—and many children (but not all) shout out the answer. Some appear to wait to hear the other children's answers. The teacher now says that the children must learn to apply what they have learned. She holds up a wooden first-aid box, and asks how much wood would be needed to construct it. The previous exercise is repeated with the new dimensions. Again, the dimensions are simple numbers. The teacher presents a third box, and tells the children that the dimensions are $7 \times 3.5 \times 4.2$ cm. She asks them to compute the surface area in their work books. She walks around the class as the children work. We also look at the work books; the children are writing out the problem in neat characters combined with numbers. They are following the format on the board. Most are getting each step right as they go along. Two or three children seem to be putting down the problem in the required steps but not computing the answers. Children use scratch paper to do the multiplication. The work books have red marks where the teacher has corrected previous lessons, and the teacher shows us with pride the work book of one child that is particularly neat. All of the red marks in this book mean "correct," and the teacher has written a character that is translated as "Excellent!"

When this exercise is completed, the teacher presents a box for Chinese chess that is produced in the school's workshop and tells the children the dimensions—$16.7 \times 16.5 \times 3.5$ cm. They again work with silent concentration in their work books. The class atmosphere is relatively relaxed; the children do not seem to be hurried or pressured, but work steadily. The fastest children finish the problem and wait for five minutes or more while the slower children are finishing. They do not turn to other work, nor talk, nor in any way disturb the still working children.

In another fourth-grade mathematics class, we watched a teacher move from formula to drawings on the board about volume with a concern for detail and an expressiveness that gave us the feeling he was unraveling a mystery. The class, too, was attentive.

Beginning at the fourth grade, in the schools we saw, children are introduced to the abacus. In one class, the teacher presented a problem, held up her hand, looking at her watch, then gave the "go" signal and the abacus on each desk began to click briskly. In our small sample, this was the only instance in which we saw the children's performance being timed. It was the consensus of the delegation that the level of arithmetic skills being taught was as high as that for children of comparable age in the United States.

A LESSON IN POLITICS: GRADE FIVE.   A woman teacher with a pleasant expression and gentle voice faces the class. The class lustily sings a Little Red Soldier song. The teacher orders crisply, "Stand!" and the children obey, shouting "Good morning" to the teacher in perfect unison. When the teacher says "Sit!" they do. The teacher then begins a lecture on Confucius. Confucius, she says, stood on the side of the slave system; he went to the Wei kingdom to organize a reaction against the rise of feudalism (which was historically progressive at that time, in terms of Marxist–Leninist historical theory).

Teacher: Is it correct that Confucius was a reactionary?
Children (in unison): It is correct!
Teacher: Did the laboring people suffer?
Children (in unison): They suffered!
Teacher: How did the workers react?
Children (in unison): They opposed him!

The teacher then asked individual children: "Who was the ruler of the Chou Kingdom?" Child names the ruler. "What was noteworthy about him?" Second child: "He was the biggest slave owner of his time." The teacher continues her lecture, explaining that Confucius fled from the Wei country and found refuge with the leader of the Chou Kingdom—proof that he was a supporter of the slave system. Confucius attempted to enter still another kingdom but was halted at the border by the people, who said that Confucius' students could enter, but not the old man himself. The aroused people said, "He is like an old dog that has no home," the phrase spoken in a contemptuous, not a sympathetic, tone.

Teacher: What did the people say about Confucius?
Children (in unison): He was like an old dog that had no home.

The teacher reports that, in order to propagate his ideas, Confucius set up a private school; she asks what some of the reactionary ideas taught there were. Individual children raise their hands, are called on, stand at their desks, and answer; "Confucius said that the cultivation and planting of crops are things done by inferior people"; "One of his students asked him if he might learn farming, and Confucius refused to allow it."

Teacher: What is this related to in our own time?

One child volunteers that it is related to Liu Shao-ch'i's revisionist line.

Teacher: Is his answer right?
Children: No!

One child volunteers that his classmate was not complete and should have added "Lin Piao."

Teacher: Why was X's answer incomplete?
Another child: We must learn from workers and soldiers.

The teacher accepts the answer and gives the children an assignment to write a paragraph on the shameful end of Confucius and why he came to it.

A LESSON IN MUSIC: GRADE THREE (AGE NINE). The children are learning a song that has been put on the blackboard in numerical notations.

6 6 6 1 2 3. 3 2̂1 1 1

The numbers replace the Western do-re-me. A dot below a number indicates a lower octave than the basic do (which is 1). A dot following a number means hold. The Chinese characters for the words are written above the numbers, and there are bar lines but no staff lines. The teacher first sings the song through, then rehearses the children phrase by phrase, demonstrating each segment and having the children repeat it. Then the whole song is sung, teacher and students in unison. Finally, the children sing the song through without the teacher. The children reach this last step in approximately fifteen minutes. The class sings lustily, with assurance. We saw few children who were not joining in.

A PHYSICAL EDUCATION CLASS. A group of sixth-grade girls is being coached in volleyball. The girls look large and strong; one would guess their age to be at least thirteen. They are wearing sweat suits. Their instructor, a rather tough-looking young man, is teaching them how to reach for a low, wide ball and how to manage if they lose their balance. The girls line up, and one by one they crouch, lunge sideways to receive the instructor's wide serve, hit the ball, and then immediately do a somersault in the dirt. Following this exercise, the instructor coaches them in receiving direct, very hard serves. They line up again, and each in turn receives the serve and returns it with her two forearms. The force of the ball is considerable, and the onlookers gasp at the loud sound of the impact of the ball against the girls' arms, but the girls maintain impassive expressions and do not flinch. The organization of the group is tight, the action is brisk. The instructor barks his instructions and uses a whistle to start each lineup.

ENGLISH LESSONS. First-year English classes are in an experimental state in Chinese primary-school education; this particular one is taught by an older teacher whose English is crisply British, accented, and grammatically accurate. Forty-seven children sit in boy–girl pairs (with one boy left over), listening to a tape recording of the day's dialogue, also in good, slightly accented English. At the end of the tape, the teacher and children recite the dialogue together and singly. Occasionally, a student gives a perfectly pronounced wrong answer to the teacher's question. She repeats the question until the correct response is given by one student or another. The second part of the lesson, which includes drawings and sentences written on the board, has to do with the tasks of workers and peasants.

Teacher: Where do workers work?
All: Workers work in the factory.
Teacher: Where do peasants work?
All: Peasants work in the field.

Teacher points to the wall poster.

Teacher: Who are they?
All: They are workers.
Teacher: What do workers do?

And so on. Then the teacher calls for "dialogue," repeating the word many times and two pairs of students, in turn, come to the front of the room and recite the lesson in unison with identical intonation and gestures.

At another school, slightly older children (apparently in their third year of English) are doing a lesson about harvesting. They read in unison from the book and then chant together the day's vocabulary:

rice	yellow	sheep	cock
cotton	white	pig	hen
time	busy	goose/geese	many
cut	happy		
pick			

At still a third school, we glanced at two English texts—an older, printed one from which the headnote to this chapter was taken and a newer, typed text with an apparently graded vocabulary about days of the week.[1] The mixture of content and procedure was striking: chanted dialogues about ideological and practical matters bring together several lines of Chinese educational practice.

A LITERATURE CLASS: GRADE THREE.   Here the teacher has been with the school for thirty years. She is a very expressive, lovely, pleasantly dramatic woman. The room is sunny, with plants growing outside the window. On the front wall is a portrait of Chairman Mao and a blackboard, on the side wall some brush writing. The children have their hands up, are bouncing up and down a little with answers to questions; they sit very straight at their desks. There is one nonresponsive little boy next to one of the delegates at the back of the room. The teacher's questions about the story in today's literature lesson are: What was the brigade like before the Revolution? What brought about all the great changes? How have the peasants managed a bumper harvest in time of drought? She answers the last question herself, "Through irrigation and digging wells." She elaborates on how the peasants make use of the rain, how they take care of their seeds, and how they struggle against natural disasters. Then she quotes a saying, that man is the decisive factor. The teacher asks what the focal point of the reading is. "Give your own reasons." A child responds but the teacher is not satisfied with the child's answer. The teacher says, *"Fighting* for what is needed is the important word in getting the good harvest." Then she points out that the second paragraph of the story is the most important because it explains how the peasants fight for a good harvest. The

1. We had hoped to bring back as complete a set of textbooks as we could collect, but because all books are said to be "in an experimental form," our hosts politely refused to let us take any examples. The best available summary in the West is in J. P. Dieny, *Le monde est à vous: la Chine et les livres pour enfants* (Paris: Gallimard, 1971).

class reads in unison. During the group reading, the teacher is alert to children who seem not to be with it; she walks up and down the aisle and corrects errors, but not in an authoritarian fashion.

Pedagogical Methods

In many of the classes we visited, demonstrations by the teacher followed by rote repetition by the students was a method generously used. Reading aloud in unison from textbooks was also common. We inquired about this, and were told that in traditional Chinese schools, this had been the primary pedagogical method, that children might be heard reciting in unison throughout the entire day. In present-day schools this practice has been much reduced, although it still is very frequent by comparison with Western practices. School officials see reducing the frequency of reading aloud in unison as an objective.

Praise for good performance is extensively used, while criticism for poor performance is relatively rare. The teacher usually does not even say that an answer given by an individual student is incorrect; frequently he or she will simply call on another student to supply a better answer. We asked about the use of punishment in the schools, and were told that once it had been widely practiced. An official of the education system of Shanghai commented,

Now we do not have punishment in our schools because the teachers have learned a lot. Their consciousness has been raised. [Question: If a child makes a mistake, what should the teacher do?] Persuade him, reason with him. We lay stress on persuasion. The teacher should try to analyze *why* the child made the mistake. She should look into his situation. Perhaps both his parents work and they have no time to teach him. If the teacher knows the reason, she can solve the problem directly. Teachers spend a lot of time getting close to the students, trying to understand them. In old China, Confucius suggested spanking the hands of children to keep discipline. I myself can remember having an old teacher who wore a small cap in school. He asked me to recite a long passage and then he went to sleep. I was mischievous and I snatched off his cap. He awoke and spanked my hands with a ruler. Punishment was very common in the old society. Children were made to stand in the corner and so on. After Liberation, the education authorities did not allow any teacher to give punishment to students.

On a number of occasions, school personnel told us with some intensity about the new educational philosophy that has prevailed since the Cultural Revolution. An experienced teacher who was involved in the supervision of younger teachers was asked what differences she could think of in teaching methods before and after the Cultural Revolution.

In the past, teaching was simple. Now the teacher not only teaches, but is a counselor, trying to help solve the difficulties of students, and also learning from the students. We used to be trained to do the thinking for the class, and let the children follow. Now we have to remember that there are forty or fifty minds within four walls, all doing the thinking. Our main job is to guide the thinking process. We pay a good deal of attention to the purpose of study. This is what really counts. The pupils are clear about this. Classes are much livelier than before. It used to be that only the teacher did the talking. Now almost every child talks. We call the new method 'elicitation.'

The "new philosophy" of education, then, reportedly calls for greater classroom participation by the students, less simple "drilling" or lecturing by the teacher. One mathematics teacher told us of asking the students, in the interests of this objective, to make up their own problems illustrating the principle being taught on a given day. Students are also supposed to be asked to volunteer their interpretations of paragraphs they read. It was our impression, however, that the interpretations they volunteered were oftentimes repetitions of interpretations supplied earlier by the teacher.

Tests. The subject of testing is heavy with politics. When we asked about testing, the school officials with whom we talked frequently assumed that we meant aptitude or I.Q. tests, and responded with the official line that no children are born stupid or bright, so testing for intellectual level is irrelevant in a socialist society. When we carefully rephrased our questions to make clear that we were referring to tests of how much the children had learned, the answer was that tests were given, but the replies of teachers continued to be guarded and qualified. We were told that many of the tests were open-book exams; and that students were encouraged to participate in making up examination questions. We did not fathom all the reasons for the uneasiness in discussing testing but assumed that tests were thought to be discriminatory against the children of workers and peasants. There is confirming evidence from other observers that the subject of examinations, particularly for entrance to the universities, remains a topic of debate and disagreement among educational leaders. The carefulness of our informants represented one of our brushes with the larger ideological debate about the virtues of being "red" over being "expert."

Productive labor

Every primary school we saw had one or more workshops. These were run in close association with a nearby factory, which supplied materials and specified the work to be done. The factory might also supply a worker to instruct and supervise the children and assist in quality control. He would be on loan to the school for a period of up to a year and a half, and might also be the worker member of the Mao Thought Propaganda Team. In some schools, this function is performed by a retired worker. The time a child spent in the workshop was geared to his age. In one primary school we visited, the children in the first two grades did not go to the workshop at all; their labor involved merely helping to clean their classrooms and sweep the courtyards. Third and fourth graders spent two class hours each week in the workshop. In grades five and six, the children spent consecutive half days for two full weeks during each term in productive labor. But work schedules varied from school to school even among the few we visited.

We saw the following kinds of work being done in primary school workshops: assembling and packaging badminton birds; painting toys; and making pieces for a game of Chinese chess, which involved a series of successive operations—shaping the edges of the wooden pieces, stamping characters on the pieces, painting and packaging—carried out by successive squads of children.

Children worked steadily at their assignments. When we came in they would smile and applaud and then return to work with occasional glances at their visitors. For the most part they worked cheerfully, although some of the older children looked slightly bored. In one workshop we saw a set of production figures on the bulletin board; for each day, the total number of items produced by each of two teams was recorded, as well as the number of imperfect items that had had to be rejected or reprocessed. The record showed increases in productivity and a decline in errors. In each workshop, one or more pupils served as monitors or inspectors, and assisted in maintaining the flow of materials. A child who ran out of raw materials for his operation would raise a hand and his monitor quickly brought more. The monitors were in turn supervised by the adult workers and teachers.

Workshops were paid by the parent factory for their products. For example, the school received approximately one cent for each set of five completed badminton birds. The money was spent for films, medicines, basketballs, and other sports equipment. In some schools, part of the money goes for costumes for the song-and-dance groups.

In addition to their work in the school workshops, the students make trips to visit nearby factories and rural communes. We were not clear on how frequent such trips are, how long the children stay, or what kind of work they do. We were told that the children are not mere onlookers during these visits, but participate actively in whatever aspects of the work of the factory or commune are suitable for their age and preparation.

Extracurricular activities

There are reported to be organized activities several times a week after school. The students have a choice among basketball, played vigorously and highly competitively by well-practiced teams; Ping-Pong; jump-rope contests; musical training, including training on both Western and traditional Chinese musical instruments, and training in more intricate choral work than is ordinarily done in the regular music classes; and art work, including needlecraft.

During the day, there are brief periods for free play (for fifteen minutes during the morning break and during part of the lunch hour if students return to school early). The after-school hours are also used for free play, although there is usually homework to be done as well. Free-play activities, in addition to basketball, jump rope, and Ping-Pong, include a game of jacks played with a knit ball that doesn't bounce and a set of bones that look like pig's knuckles, a game we saw played only by girls.

Student organization

Every class has several class leaders. Some of these are leaders of the Little Red Soldiers (described in more detail later); others are all-class leaders, elected by the students and serving for one term (six months). The duties of the class leaders include traditional American monitor functions—taking care of classroom equipment, helping to keep discipline, and assigning cleanup jobs. In the marching exercises during calisthenics, student leaders serve as drill sargeants and call out marching orders. At one setting, a student lead the whole school in the midmorning calisthenics.

The group of children who occupy class leadership positions meets regularly with the teacher. They take responsibility for trying to help other children in the class who are having difficulty with their schoolwork or with settling down to the expected classroom regimen. An example was given of a child who was a good student but broke classroom discipline by answering the teacher's questions immediately without raising his hand. The group of student leaders in his class had a talk with him, explaining that his behavior made it impossible for the teacher to call on some of the slower students first, so that he was interfering with their learning. The student leaders stressed that he should be trying to help other students learn, and should be less concerned with displaying his own knowledge. The members of the leadership group took turns reminding the recalcitrant student (reportedly in a friendly way) just before he entered the classroom each morning that it was important to raise his hand to be called on. The student's behavior improved and his class leaders congratulated him publicly.

We asked whether a child ever resented this kind of surveillance and control from his classmates. We were told that children usually accepted such criticism with good grace, but that occasionally a child would flare up and walk out of a group criticism meeting. The student leadership group would then ask the teacher to talk with the child and, sometimes, his parents.

THE LITTLE RED SOLDIERS.   Most of our information on China's organization for primary-school children, the Little Red Soldiers, was obtained in an interview with two coaches of the organization, Li Ku-yin and Liu Pei-tzu, both teachers at a primary school attached to the Shanghai Normal School. Almost all the children in grades three through six are members of the Little Red Soldiers, and an effort is currently under way to recruit at the second-grade level. We were told that in other schools Little Red Soldiers may be inducted as early as the second half of the first year and that there is some variation in age on induction across the country. In the Shanghai school, approximately half the pupils in grade three are members and over 90 percent of the students are members by grade six. Sixth-grade Little Red Soldiers welcome new first-graders by decorating their classrooms and providing some information about the organization and its requirements so that the "little ones will have a good feeling toward the Little Red Soldiers and will be eager to join as soon as possible." Pupils who do not make it by grade six are encouraged to keep trying and to apply for admission to the Red Guards in middle school.

The Little Red Soldiers, according to our informants, had their origins before Liberation. As new areas were taken over by Communists, children's brigades were formed to help the Red Army. The children served as guards, and were armed with little spears. They also carried messages. Shortly after 1949 a new organization was formed, called the Young Pioneers. They were dedicated to "love of country, aiding the socialist revolution, and help in socialist construction" by salvaging scrap iron and assisting work in factories. After the Cultural Revolution, the Young Pioneers were reorganized as the Little Red Soldiers.

After repeated questions about the differences between the Young Pioneers and the Little Red Soldiers, and quite a bit of untranslated discussion between the coaches, our interpreter reported that the Young Pioneers used to continue into the middle school, but now the Little Red Soldiers ended with primary school, with the Red Guard organization taking over in the middle school. "We do not say that the Young Pioneers were bad; there are some connections. It is a continuous step. The Little Red Soldiers were the result of the Cultural Revolution; Liu Shao-Ch'i's revisionist line appeared in the Pioneers and so there had to be a change. Still, Little Red Soldiers wear the same red scarf."

According to Ms. Li, the purpose of the Little Red Soldiers is "not only to educate the young pupils about our tradition, but to expose them to good deeds at the present time, and especially to carry out Chairman Mao's directive for good health, study, and productive work—'the three goods.' " We were told that in each primary school there was a corps composed of platoons, one for each classroom, the platoons being further broken down into squads. Although the term "corps" was universal, the subdivisions at other schools around the country might be called brigades, teams, or detachments. The corps is always under the leadership of the school's Youth League branch and is under the local Party branch. The corps is governed by a committee composed of one representative from every class. For example, in Ms. Li's school, the committee was composed of nineteen members, one from each platoon. There are usually four squads in each platoon, one for each row, and squad membership is determined by chance, but rows are rotated during the term. When we asked why, we were told that this was so that children in a given row wouldn't always be looking in one direction, "to protect the eyes."

Each corps has a commander and two deputy commanders, but their functions are largely ceremonial. The principal leadership comes from the corps committee, which is divided into four groups, each carrying responsibility for planning in one area. The political and propaganda group organizes political education and circulates propaganda materials; the labor committee plans activities for the workshops and farm typically attached to each school; the organization group recruits new members and makes periodic evaluations of the entire membership through the mechanisms of group criticism and self-criticism; and the recreation group plans physical culture, song, and dance.

The members of the corps committee are divided into these four groups without overlapping. The commander and the two deputy commanders serve on different subgroups. In each subgroup, the representative from the oldest grade acts as chairman. This arrangement provides an opportunity for younger members to be trained for the chairman's role over the years. Members are chosen through group discussion leading to consensus and without formal election. It is possible for the same child to remain on the executive committee for several years.

The organization of the platoon parallels that of the corps, with seven to nine children acting as members of a governing committee, subdivided into the same four functions, but now with only one to three members assigned to each activity.

The corps committee meets twice a week for political study of Chairman Mao's work, and for learning and discussion. The adult leaders attend some but not all of the meetings. At the end of each semester the corps leader holds a meeting of the entire Little Red Soldier organization in the school to hear reports and criticism on the work done. Beforehand there is always a meeting of the platoon leaders, which in turn has had information funneled to it from meetings at the squad level. Through this system outstanding performance or problem behavior on the part of individual pupils is brought to general attention.

We were told, for example, that this year it was discovered that "the sixth grade platoon leader in charge of physical labor had come early every morning to get everything ready, and had stayed afterwards to clean up. This same platoon leader had visited the homes of twenty-one of his classmates' families to see the homes in which they lived and to help those who lagged behind in their work."

Similar meetings are held at the level of the platoon and the squad, both of which have leaders and deputy leaders. Our informants told us that at a recent platoon meeting one of the children reported, "The other night when I got home I couldn't remember what my assignment was. Just then there was a knock at the door and there was my squad leader to remind me about the assignment and help me work on it."

A second pupil recounted another incident. "Just as school was closing, it began to rain heavily. One of the squad leaders dashed out into the rain and soon returned with umbrellas for the children." When we asked the coaches whether these stories were made up as ideal examples to follow, or whether they described real events, we were assured they actually happened.

Using as an example the slogan of the American Boy Scouts, "Be prepared," we asked whether the Little Red Soldiers had any slogans or guiding principles. "We do not have slogans but our aim is clear—to unite to become masters of the country, to study, to develop morally, intellectually, and physically. We are concerned with practice, not words."

The corps committee meets once a week to give direction to platoon activities. Some meetings are devoted to criticism and self-criticism. Children who have "done good deeds" are reported to the school and sometimes to the parents.

Last month we had some activities devoted to the theme of hard work. In connection with this theme, we visited the Good Eighth Company of Nanking Road, and talked with the uncles of the company. One of the pupils, T'an Shan-li, was deeply moved by this experience. For some time, he had been asking his parents for a new bookcase because his old one was dilapidated, but after visiting with the PLA uncles he decided to repair the old one. His comrades learned of the change and announced it over the school broadcasting system and put it on the blackboard. T'an Shan-li is in the fifth grade, twelve years old.

We asked how his classmates had learned of his change of mind. "They had heard him talking before about wanting a new bookcase, and then saw him repairing the old one."
We were given a second example.

Last October 1, our national day, the school organized some activities devoted to the theme of the treasures of our seas. We set ourselves the task of showing the beauty of the sea, but we had no treasures. So the children brought things from home. Everyone made a contribution. Some of the children drew pictures day and night. Comments were made afterward on who had been the most unselfish, and letters of praise were sent to the families of these children.

When we asked for examples of criticism, we were told that criticism was always combined with praise.

A fourth grader who was a cadre member passed by a piece of waste paper without picking it up. A monitor noticed this and told him he should pick it up. He said, "I didn't drop it." The monitor reported the incident to the corps committee, which in turn called a meeting of all its members at which the fourth grader was criticized, and then made an appropriate self-criticism.

Revisionist ideas are still around. For example, the first week of school we went to help with the harvest. The Little Red Soldiers picked over the fields that had already been harvested, to collect any seedlings that had been overlooked, so that nothing would be wasted. One of the children found some manure. Some of the children turned away from it saying it had a bad smell, but one child picked it up and preserved it for fertilizer. This incident was made the subject of a general meeting at which it was pointed out that the fragrance of the grain came from hard labor and from the ill-smelling fertilizer that was put on it.

Sometimes criticism of one class is initiated by another. For example, two sixth-grade classes had adjacent farming plots. Members of one class sometimes walked across the other's plot to get to their own. As a result of a complaint by the second class, the first class had a self-criticism meeting. It was pointed out that their behavior was not in accordance with the values of the PLA uncles, who treat every plant as their own. Following their self-criticism, the children plowed the plot of the other class and built a fence around it so that no one would take the shortcut in the future.

We asked about selection and recruitment of Little Red Soldiers. At this particular school, selection begins in the second grade. Little Red Soldiers in the sixth grade visit the second grade to explain the purposes of the organization and ask pupils to apply. The application must include self-criticism as well as comments from other classmates and from the sixth graders. These nominations are then sent to the corps committee, which makes the final decision. In the upper grades, the decisions are made from within the class itself.

We had earlier obtained some information about the Little Red Soldiers in an interview with two coaches in another Shanghai primary school. They described for us the Little Red Soldiers in their school. The first activity, they said, began at seven-thirty in the morning, when the pupils began lining up in front of the school. It was the duty of twenty Little Red Soldiers to make sure that the lineup was orderly. The lineup was followed by morning exercises. Then, at eight o'clock, there was a special Little Red Soldiers' period involving discussions of current affairs, moral behavior, hygienic practices, and some criticism and self-criticism. We asked what the topics had been on the previous day. "We discussed how the workers and peasants have to fight the natural forces of the river and asked the children to learn from the workers and peasants." Then the children were given the four do's and don't's of health and hygiene.

Do's
1. Wash your hair and get a haircut.
2. Brush your teeth.
3. Take a bath and change your clothes.
4. Wash your hands and cut nails.

Don't's
1. Don't drink unboiled water.
2. Don't eat unclean food.
3. Don't spit.
4. Don't litter.

The children were also told to protect their eyes by abiding by four rules: sit straight when reading or writing; keep your reading or work at a distance of one and a half feet; rest after reading for an hour by looking into the distance; don't read lying in bed, in the bathtub, or while walking.

When we asked about moral instruction, we were told that the previous day the children had heard a story about a Little Red Soldier in grade three who wanted a new pen. His father agreed but then gave him an old pen. The child complained that his classmates would laugh at him, which they did. But then the father told his son that the pen had actually belonged to a hero of the revolution. It was a hero's pen. Learning of this fact, the son was no longer disappointed, and his classmate's laughter turned to admiration. The children were then told about the duty of Little Red Soldiers to show concern for their classmates, to help younger students (remember, these were third-graders) to cut their fingernails and learn to read and write, and persuade them not to quarrel. Our informants then reported that when the children were asked for examples of good deeds done by members, they told of a Little Red Soldier who had visited a sick classmate, brought him an exercise book, and helped him go over work he had missed. Another was described as giving lessons in arithmetic to twelve other children.

The reply to our request for examples of criticized behavior was long in Chinese but short in English: "Chairman Mao says, 'Except in a desert, there is always a left, a middle, and a right.' This means that some pupils are not strict with themselves and don't have a fighting spirit, don't study well, and don't show concern for classmates." We asked about qualifications for membership in the Little Red Soldiers and were told that they consisted of concern with current affairs, service to the people, studying hard, showing a spirit of self-criticism and criticism, and taking an active part in physical education.

SMALL GROUPS. We were told that primary-school teachers help to organize small groups of children in the same class who live near one another to study together after school. The groups are made up of varying numbers of children, apparently seldom as many as ten, and one child is identified as the group leader. These groups meet together at the home of one of the children; the teacher takes care to see that at least one of the children has grandparents at home, so that there will be a place for them to meet that will have adult supervision. The group leader's job is to see to it that all the children know what their assignments are and that they complete their homework. We interviewed one nine-year-old girl who was the leader of a three-child study group. We asked her whether they could play after school. She said firmly and fiercely, *"First* we do our homework, *then* we play." Up until approximately the third or fourth grade, the small groups are mixed as to sex. After this, by the student's own choice (so the teachers and parents say) they become all-girl or all-boy groups.

Relationships between teachers and students

We were repeatedly told that nowadays there is a democratic and friendly rather than authoritarian relationship between teachers and students. In theory, the children have a right to criticize their teachers. If a teacher punishes a child in class, for example, the children explicitly has the right to put up a "big character poster"—the method of denouncing someone who is guilty of incorrect thought or action. We did not, however, hear of an instance in which this had actually been done. The children seemed generally very respectful and courteous in their behavior toward the teachers. We never saw a case of rudeness or defiance. At the same time, the children did not seem to be in fear of the teachers. A friendly, work-oriented atmosphere usually prevailed; the teachers seemed pleased with their children's successes and the children seemed to feel gratified by the teachers' appreciation. We saw easy conversation between teachers and children outside of classes with occasional affectionate gestures.

We do not know whether this atmosphere was created especially to impress foreign visitors. One of us did go back to an art class to pick up some drawings, making an unexpected visit at a time when the class was not in formal session but when several students were still present in the room. The teacher appeared harrassed and was speaking to the children in sharp tones, which were moderated when the visitor appeared. The "new-style" teacher–student relationships obviously cannot be universal in the Chinese schools. Our limited observations that there may be some stubborn obstacles to criticizing teachers seem confirmed by an article that appeared in *People's Daily* shortly after our visit. A Little Red Soldier, stimulated by a performance put on by some middle-school Red Guards, wrote in her "diary" some comments critical of how her teacher was treating students. These diaries are not diaries as we understand them, but techniques for students to report their thoughts; the teacher read the girl's diary and was upset. She retaliated by criticizing the girl, and led other students in criticizing her for such things as "attacking the prestige of teachers." The girl stuck to her guns but was troubled; she became unable to eat and had nightmares. Finally, she wrote a letter to the editor of *People's Daily* asking if she had in fact committed an error—to which the newspaper responded, of course, that it was the teacher who was in the wrong.

Observations concerning the "personalities" of primary-school children

At the meetings we had with school personnel, student leaders were also present, and they did not hesitate to speak up when the discussion touched on a topic to which they could contribute. The children were usually excited by the presence of foreign visitors, but they were neither shy nor inclined to show off. On several occasions, a student leader would come forward with a little speech of friendship for the American people, or would present us with some children's drawings or a product from the school's workshop. These presentations were done with style and self-confidence. When we observed extracurricular activities children challenged us to games of Ping-Pong, and enjoyed winning, but were careful to moderate their spectacular games so as not to make us look as incompetent as we were—"Friendship first, competition second."

A question we tried to answer in observing children at school was whether or not the children were paying a psychological price for the relatively high levels of discipline, academic demands, and peer conformity to pressure that prevailed. On the basis of the evidence available to us there were few signs of unhealthy adjustment. School health authorities reported a very low level of psychosomatic disorders, absentee rates were extraordinarily low, and the children generally appeared to us to be cheerful and goal-oriented; their demeanor was self-confident. Our impression of primary-school students, more limited in range and number, mirrored our impression of kindergartners—that obvious signs of tension, depression, or apathy were rare compared to those in groups of Western children.

Of course, there may be adverse consequences at a deeper level than we were able to observe. In every classroom, when the teacher asked a question, a large number of hands would go up, but there were always some children who did not volunteer. There may have been some children who were in this unready group repeatedly. Were they unmotivated? Did they feel anxiety over their academic weakness? Perhaps more crucial, what about the 10 percent of the children who had not gained admission to the Little Red Soldiers by the end of the sixth grade? We were told that in their individual conferences, children who were not yet judged ready for admission were always told about the areas in which they had made progress, and were encouraged to feel that with a few improvements they *could* be admitted. Did these children continue to work with positive morale? Or did they become discouraged after trying year after year and never being quite good enough? We do not know. These problems beset some children in every culture. The issue is whether the Chinese system produces an especially large number of them and how an unsuccessful person is made to feel by those around him. We heard often that one must never heap scorn upon a weaker or less able person than oneself, but must stand ready to help, and must attempt to discover what this person *can* do that will enable him to serve the interests of the society. But achievement motivation is so high and so pervasive, it is difficult for American psychologists to believe that the low-achievement child does not suffer acutely for his failures. All we can say is that the large majority of children appeared to our foreign eyes to be positively engaged by the system.

INDIVIDUAL DIFFERENCES.   As we have already remarked, the official Chinese ideology is that there are no innate differences in intelligence. When we inquired about "exceptional" children, we were told about special schools for the deaf or the blind, but not about special facilities for retarded children. Indeed, our Chinese translators could not find a good word for "retarded children" in Chinese and communication on the topic was especially difficult. Teachers were ready enough to discuss the fact that some children were better prepared for schooling than others and that some seemed to learn faster. After every test, we were told, it would be evident that some children were not up to the expected level. The school authorities would then ask the teachers to analyze the reasons. In general, four classes of reasons for a child being slow are recognized:

Parents do not understand the importance of study: because some parents have not been to school themselves, they do not tell their children how to study.

The child is not concentrating on his work, because he lacks a clear purpose. An example was given of a boy who was known to be very clever but failed an examination. The boy was then helped to think about why he was going to school.

The child has missed some necessary preparatory work, because of illness, moving, or some other reason. In this case, the teacher gives makeup tutoring outside of class.

For some other reason, the child simply has difficulty learning. Fewer academic demands are made of such a student. Official policy is clearly opposed to tracking of any sort, however. Before the Cultural Revolution, if a child failed an important set of examinations he was simply kept back without further analysis. The children to whom this happened would be in low spirits, would feel inferior. Nowadays, we were told, more effort is made to help and encourage such students, and the whole class participates. The teacher makes clear to everyone that nobody should despise a slow student, that every person can contribute in his own way. Special coaching and "cooperation with the parents" are undertaken whenever a child is seen as having some "weakness." As a rough criterion, we were told, the number of repeaters should not exceed 1 percent of the children. If it does, the teacher has probably not done sufficient analysis to identify the children whose slowness is due to the first two reasons. An extremely slow child who does not seem able to learn even with special tutoring would be held back and not promoted with his age-mates if the parents requested it, but the teachers stressed that this was very rare indeed. In one large primary school, the teachers could only remember one child (now in the third grade) who had continued to have serious learning problems; they agreed that there might be one such child in the present first grade, but they were working hard to try to bring him up to an acceptable level of performance.

We had little success in communicating the concept of hyperactivity. We would describe the symptoms and first-grade teachers would agree that some children, especially those who had not attended kindergarten, might have some difficulty in settling down to the routine of a classroom; such difficulty, they said, might last as long as three weeks or even a month. For restless children (usually boys), the main task was to guide them "to be good according to Chairman Mao." Chronic hyperactivity, however, was simply not a familiar problem to them nor to teachers of higher grades.

We told the teachers we had noticed that when an assignment was given for an arithmetic problem to be done in class, some students finished considerably sooner than others. We asked whether any extra work was given to the fastest students to keep them busy. The teachers said that if a student did learn very easily, he was put to work helping to coach the slower students.

We asked whether it was easier or harder to teach home-reared children than children who had previously been exposed to a collective setting in nurseries and kindergartens. Unlike our sample of kindergarten teachers, the primary teachers held consistent opinions on the point: home-reared children were considered to be somewhat more difficult to teach initially because they had not had instruction in numbers and other elements of basic knowledge that were needed for first-grade work and because they were "spoiled" —not accustomed to group living and the behavioral controls required thereby. In one school there was an explicit program of special coaching during the first few weeks of the first grade aimed at bringing the home-reared children up to the level of the kinder-garten-trained children. We asked how long the differences be-tween the two groups persisted; the teachers did not agree fully on this, but the most common opinion was that it did not last beyond the first year of primary school.

Teacher selection and training

Our picture of the processes of teacher selection and training is incomplete, and most of what we know has to do with teachers trained in university normal schools, probably a very small pro-portion of whom ever teach at the primary level.

In each of the schools we visited, we inquired about additions to the staff and the training that had been received by the most recently added teachers. The general picture was that the large majority of teachers were trained and hired by the schools before 1966. There appears to have been very little staff turnover since that time. We do not know how staffing was accomplished for any schools that were opened during the 1966–73 hiatus. Because the schools we visited were all well-established prior to the Cultural Revolution, they may have presented a picture of much greater faculty stability and upper-level training than would be the case in a more representative group of schools.

Summary note

Even more than in the case of our kindergarten observations, we felt that the primary schools we saw, and perhaps the students in them, represented an unusual sample of the Chinese range—the very best, perhaps. Still, nothing we saw led us to modify markedly the portrait of Chinese education that we had begun to sketch earlier. The uniformity and discipline of classrooms were more visible in primary schools than in kindergarten. In addition, the important role of systematic and guided peer influence is vividly seen in the work of classroom officers, the Little Red Soldiers, the ideology of preparing the young "to take over," and the apparent hesitancy to subject teachers to criticism. The restriction of the curriculum to the practical and the avoidance of the theoretical begins to be apparent; it will become commanding in middle school. American visitors could not fail to notice the infrequency, even in these showplace schools, of problem-solving exercises, intellectual exchange among students, and skeptical questioning. And, for some of us, the charm and skill of kindergartners in song and dance and drawing began, in the primary schools, to show the limitations of imitative copying and the unyielding requirements of established patterns.

In our short observation of primary schools, we saw the continuing development of children who were expressive, lively, remarkably self-controlled, generally committed to their tasks, and without the disorders of behavior we have come to expect at a steady low base rate in American schools—hyperactivity, impulsivity, isolated withdrawal, and neurotic symptoms. We are even less sure in our guesses about primary-school teachers; we saw so few, in such showcase circumstances, that we can only circumspectly note their apparent briskness, competence, and interest in their tasks.

Some interesting sidelights on problem-solving and cooperative behavior among second-graders and teachers' perceptions of that behavior were obtained in a brief demonstration with a Western apparatus. One of us brought to China a Mintz Jar—a clear plastic jar with a hose for admitting water into the lower portion of the jar, and a single "escape hatch" at the top through which wooden "men," attached to strings, can be withdrawn one at a time. The procedure typically used is as follows: three children at one time hold the ends of three strings, and at a "go" signal, each attempts to get his man out through the escape hatch. If the three subjects pull simultaneously, the wooden men jam at the neck of the exit, and none can be withdrawn. If the subjects work out a strategy of pulling out in an arranged order, all three men can be removed before the water rises high enough to get them wet. In the elementary school in Peking where this apparatus was used, the "game" was first demonstrated to a group of teachers and the principal. All were interested and excited. One teacher suggested that when the apparatus was brought into the classroom, the wooden men should already be inside—if the students saw the men being put in, it would be too obvious to them that they could only pass through the opening one at a time. Another teacher suggested that the jar should be partly filled with water before the "go" signal, to reduce the decision time and make the problem more difficult. The game was introduced to a class of eight-year-old children in the following way.

> These men [pointing to the wooden pieces on strings] are building a tunnel; a leak has started and the water is rising; the men must get out of the tunnel before the water reaches them. Each of you [three children] will hold a string, and must try to pull your man out quickly as soon as I say 'go.'

The experimenter asked for three girls; the teacher asked for volunteers and many hands went up. The teacher selected three girls, who came to the front of the room and each took the end of a string. The girls then began to whisper among themselves who was to go first, who second, who third. At the go signal they followed their plan neatly and got all three men out in minimal time.

The experimenter then suggested repeating the procedure with three boys. The teacher was doubtful, saying that since the whole class had seen what happened on the first trial, they would already be alerted to the solution. However, the boys were eager to try the game, so the teacher called on three of them. They accepted the strings without consultation with each other. At the "go" signal, one reacted very quickly and got his man out. The other two jammed at the exit. Then one boy (who was wearing a red scarf) said softly to the other, "This is dangerous; you go first and I'll go after you." He then released his string and allowed the other boy's wooden man to exit, then pulled his out.

The teacher then put her arm around the boy's shoulder, and turned him to face the class, saying, "It was good of you to let the other one go first; now you see what it means to be a Little Red Soldier."

A foundry in a middle school outside Sian. The molten metal is poured into pots and carried to earth molds inside the foundry. Students carry on all parts of the melting and casting procedures under the direction of a worker–advisor.

A middle-school laboratory exercise in Science (or rather, in Common Knowledge of Industry and Agriculture). Equipment is limited, the exercises always have practical implications, and the students seem zealous in their attention.

On days when the Sian Foreign Language Institute students are not working with the peasants at the dam, they continue their studies; here they study English.

6. THE MIDDLE SCHOOL

The proletarian class thinks that education should serve the people and strengthen Marxism–Leninism–Mao Tse-tung thought.

—Briefing at Peking Middle School #31

Once again, our sample of middle schools was too small to warrant even a parody of generalization. We visited three middle schools after our urgent request to look in on higher secondary education and, although we heard about middle schools and their students in a number of briefings and in our less formal conversations with our hosts, the commentary that makes up the present chapter must carry even more heavily underlined reservations than were necessary for our observations about primary school. And not merely because our data base is so narrow: two touchy issues arise with Chinese middle schools that make summary difficult—general availability of middle-school education and procedures for selecting students.

We were told that from enrollments of less than a million before 1949, there has been steady and dramatic increase, to 5 million in 1956 and to 35 million in 1972. Because some middle schools have only recently reopened after the shutdowns of the Cultural Revolution, because there is variation in the number of years spent in middle school (four, five, or even six), and, finally, because recent population statistics are not available, it is difficult to guess how many members of the appropriate age group attend middle school. On the crude assumption that primary school is about as long as middle school, Hsiao Ching-jo's assertion of enrollments of 127 and 35 million in the two systems testifies to the constriction of accessibility of education that takes place for children between twelve and eighteen years of age. One may speculate, on our own and other evidence, that there is the usual variation between city and country, that there are many more children in junior (first two or three years) than in senior middle schools, and that there continues to be active debate in China about the duration, curriculum, and administration of middle schools.

Our information about selection for middle school—especially, for upper middle school—is, if anything, even more problematic. We were told that in the old days admission was by examination and that the particular middle school a student attended depended on his standing in the examinations. As more and more primary school graduates can enter junior middle school, it was said, such examinations have become less and less necessary; since the Cultural Revolution, schools have not been organized by examination level. When we asked what selection procedures were used when they were still necessary, we were told, on one occasion, that admission was decided by the needs of the state. A more specific answer was given in a Sian school that serves a somewhat rural population. Fourteen classes of senior-middle-school students were drawn from a wide geographical area; some students even had to be boarded at the school. Priority for admission was given to children of poor and lower-middle peasants; a good recommendation was required both from the student's junior middle school and from the production brigade in which he did his productive labor; and, finally, admission examinations were conducted by the school. In an urban school (Peking #31), we were told that 60 percent of the parents of the students were workers, 30 percent were staff and cadre, 6 percent were military, and 2 percent, "former capitalists." In our briefings, emphasis was always laid on the importance of class origin and earlier service rather than on grades and examinations as criteria for admission. We cannot say to what degree the apparent contest between old and new procedures for admission has been resolved or compromised. We remain uneasy about the representativeness of our observations with regard either to all Chinese children of the appropriate age cohort or even just to those who are in middle schools.

Physical plant and faculty

The middle schools we visited varied somewhat in plant. In Peking, the middle-school buildings had been part of a British private school before 1949. The buildings were relatively small, close to one another, with a large central court or assembly yard. Some of the workshops and laboratories, in what were formerly the dormitories of the school, were in a rather poor state and some were being repaired or enlarged. The middle school in Shanghai consisted of several two- and three-story brick buildings facing a large assembly yard and was much more compact than the Peking school. The Sian suburban school had a true campus, a series of brick buildings on a steep hillside, built before 1949. Interspersed with the classroom buildings were long walkways, a library, and dormitories still in use. At the bottom of the hill were a factory, workshops, orchards, gardens, and pigsties. We were told that the Sian school provided food for some students, but in the other middle schools, the students were said to go home for lunch.

The enrollment was said to be 1,800 in the Peking school, 1,900 in Sian, and 2,600 in Shanghai; the teacher–student ratio varied between 1:20 and 1:26 depending on the distinction our hosts made between teachers and staff. The size of most of the classes we saw was just over 50 students, each class with one teacher. The reported teacher–student ratio, then, suggests that teachers are not engaged in classroom work for most of the day. We were told (in Sian) that most teachers spend about ten to twelve hours a week in the classroom and the rest of their workday in preparation, grading papers, working with single students or small groups, and visits to the homes of their students.

Educational philosophy and curriculum

The general structure and content of the briefings we heard on the educational philosophy of middle schools did not depart in most respects from what we had heard about other levels of Chinese schooling. We were reminded that children were not the

private property of the family, and that schooling was for production and political education as well as for cultural education,
that students learned "to contribute to society, to serve the people wholeheartedly, and to advance production, class struggle,
and scientific research."

The intimate and necessary connection between theory and
practice has been, we were told, even more at the center of the
curriculum since the Cultural Revolution. We were told of Mao's
anecdotes about educated youth who could not distinguish one
crop from another or fix their own broken light fixtures. "If you
plow your fields on the blackboard, you get no crop." "Students
are taught that it is important to build their country by their own
hands and to create a spirit of self-reliance; students learn from
books, but they also learn to criticize the bourgeoisie and to love
physical labor."

Among the schools we saw, there seemed to be a fairly consistent pattern of schedule. Students spend about eight months in
school proper, one month in productive agricultural labor or in a
factory, and two months of apparently supervised vacation, one
month in midwinter and one in midsummer. Again, apparently as
a general pattern, the students' eight-hour day runs from eight
until four and is divided into six forty-minute classroom periods,
a midmorning exercise period, and a lunch break. As in the
primary schools, there were organized and supervised after-school
activities going on in all three schools.

So far as we could tell, the middle-school curriculum is fixed
for all students and is made up of courses in Chinese language,
politics, mathematics, physics, chemistry (these two sometimes
called "common knowledge of industry and agriculture"), history,
geography, foreign language (reportedly most often English, then
Russian, then other Western languages), and physical exercise;
music and drawing get their major emphasis outside regular class
hours. The schools we visited, according to report, taught mathematics in an integrated and always practical form, with no separation by level into algebra, geometry, and trigonometry.

Let us again escape somewhat from the awesome statistical

limitations on us by recounting stories about what we saw.

A Chinese-language class (Peking). The students are writing a report today about a blind man who visited them yesterday. Small groups of six or eight children discuss what impressed them about the visit; then each of the children is to write an essay. The teacher says, "Your compositions may be about your impressions or your feelings, or it may be a summary of the report made by the blind man." One of us joined a table of three boys and three girls.

Boy 1: The blind man asked for help in learning the ways of Chairman Mao.

Girl 1: Why does he do it? He must have some inner spirit.

Girl 2: Yes, we must work hard continuously our whole lives; we can't stop.

Girl 3: One thing more; he not only studies well by himself, but he helps organize others. This is important for us—in class and collectively.

The third girl then criticized herself, saying that, because she lived farther from school than the others, she missed certain meetings on snowy nights. That was wrong.

Boy 2: Blind men in olden times were beggars or fortune tellers and the rich sent dogs to bite them. Now a blind man is honored to come to our school and to tell us of his struggles and success.

Girl 1: A blind man will meet many difficulties in life. If he overcomes difficulties, why can't we?

Boy 1: This blind man is making boxes in a factory; he is not just a consumer.

Boy 3: From 1964 on, the blind man organized a study group. Study must supercede other interests.

A chemistry class (Peking). The teacher has brought a test-tube experiment to class; he explains and demonstrates the experiment in front of the classroom. The class of about fifty students listens and takes notes. The students are assigned laboratory experiments to do on their own and we see them working in pairs in the laboratory. Equipment is sparse and old; the books used emphasize practical applications of chemistry.

An English class (Peking). The text used for third-year English is a paperbound book of eighty pages; each of some ten chapters has a short essay, followed by questions in English that call for factual answers. At the end of each chapter is a section on grammar (part English, part Chinese) and a group of exercises in English on verb forms, idiomatic expressions, and so on. The class is reading a story.

Driving for the Revolution

Hsiao Liu is sent to the countryside. He wants to drive a tractor; he is disappointed because he must drive a wagon with mules. But an older worker explains the teachings of Chairman Mao. "The harder we work, the more energetic we feel." We should not choose revolutionary work but should let revolutionary work choose us. Hsiao Liu is so impressed that he says he will drive his wagon right through the Revolution.

The class was drilled in traditional recitational style, reading and rereading the paragraph aloud. The teacher used only English in conducting the class. While the students read aloud one of us leafed through the book, apparently published in 1973. There were a few fables—"The Wolf in Sheep's Clothing" and "The Boy Who Cried Wolf"—a few stories about the exploits of factories, shipyards, and of individual workers, and at least three stories about young heroes who fooled the "Yanks" in Viet Nam. One boy volunteers to go down to a dry well to search for weapons for a group of "Yank bandits" that come to his village searching for members of the People's Liberation Army. The Americans are glad to get him to do this dirty work, but when he comes up he throws a hand grenade into their midst, killing them all. The reading ends by observing that the brave people of Viet Nam will never give up their country to the imperialist bandits.

Later, the teacher asked the delegate to tape record a few of the stories, so the children could improve their pronunciation. We started with "The Wolf in Sheep's Clothing," then moved on to "An Industrial Exhibition," extolling new production techniques. "A Small Yard Builds a Big Ship" told how, by using Chairman Mao's teachings, "we built a 10,000-ton ship in our little repair yard." Deftly the teacher skipped a chapter dealing with Viet Nam and asked one of us to record a chapter in which a foreign visitor tells how impressed he is with developments in China and with the hospitality he has received.

Physical exercise. There are school-wide midmorning physical drills for twenty minutes daily in the assembly area outdoors. The students line up for mass drill; a teacher (and on occasion a student) directs the drill with a microphone from a raised platform. During the exercises, music for marching is played over the loudspeaker.

Eye exercises are also done by the group. We saw these once in large assembly; another time, they were performed in class. The exercises to prevent myopia, continued from primary school, consist of pressure and massage, in specified ways, around the bone socket of the eyes.

Politics ("social investigation"). Students are encouraged to use their spare time (including Sundays and vacations) to "merge themselves with the people" and to gather material for school reports. Sometimes a team of students carries out a joint project of this kind.

At Sian, students investigated social changes since 1949 and learned, along the way, that of ninety students, thirty had parents who were hired out before the present regime and that, in their own school, girls used not to be admitted. Teachers and administrators reported that students were inspired by such before-and-after investigations.

Students in the Peking school told us that during the preceding month, a group of them had made a nine-day visit to the countryside for an investigation. Their project was organized in response to some questions raised by students at the school. Why should they study science when they were destined simply to become peasants and do manual labor? The purpose of the project was to find out whether scientific knowledge was useful in the countryside. They talked to groups of "educated sent-down youth" who had graduated from middle school. They asked for instances in which they had applied their knowledge, or in which they found they needed *more* knowledge. They were told about some young people who were given the assignment of spreading fertilizer. They spread too much, because they did not know its chemical composition, and burned the plants. In another instance, when some irrigation pumps broke down, there was no one who knew how to repair them. The Peking student research team noted that they had already studied in school about how to repair pumps, and they knew they would be better prepared than the previous students had been to meet such problems. The students reported their findings to their fellow students, stressing that what they learned in school was needed—that there is never enough knowledge to meet all the problems of mechanization, irrigation, electrification, and fertilization that are encountered in the countryside.

Later, we asked the director and staff to tell us about the practical significance of foreign-language study. Without hesitation, they related an instance in which village peasants had been sent packages of improved seed from America but could not read the planting instructions. A middle-school graduate could have helped them.

Productive labor. At least two kinds of regular school-supervised labor programs exist. One is the physical labor at the school in workshops. The other is the month-long off-campus work that students do in communes or in factories.

Each year, the student spends one month of six hours per day (six days per week) in school workshops. In Peking, the shops were building electric circuits for trucks, printing, making printed circuits, assembling amplifiers, and operating a machine tool shop. These shops had the help of a retired worker and of a master worker from a factory, as well as of their teachers. Also in Peking middle schools, students, with the help of adults from the communes to which the school sends its students for agricultural-month assignments, were building new workshops. In the Sian workshops, factory and agricultural units, the students were welding, doing carpentry, raising pigs and chickens, making hot pourings for casting machine parts, and turning machine tool parts on a metal lathe. Students in the middle school (which we did not visit) of the Peking Textile Mill complex were said to be brought to the mill itself for short work experiences.

Each year, middle-school students also put in a stint of work away from school. They are said to go on marches, some of them several hundred kilometers in length, which take them to the sites of their labor assignments. They apparently go by class and the work may be in either an agricultural or an industrial setting.

Music and dance. If the Peking middle school we visited was representative of large urban schools, performances of music and dance are a consequential part of education. In the Peking school, we were told that there is a yearly school-wide performance in which about 1,000 of the 1,800 students take part, and that there are about 140 smaller performances during a year. Performances are reportedly designed to reflect feelings, not to demand excellence. Students give these performances for themselves, for parents, and for the workers and peasants. We were told, too, that parts of the performance are composed or created by the students themselves.

In Peking, the school "propaganda team"—composed of students who apparently have special musical and dance skills, was practicing after school for a performance to be given at the factory allied with the school. They were preparing orchestral work, accordion and piano solos, vocal solos, and dance. As usual, the content was overwhelmingly ideological—"To the People of Taiwan," "Praise Peking," "Our Friends all over the World."

At the Sian middle school the students' performance included orchestral music, song, and dance. It had the same political flavor, plus an American folksong, Clementine. The Sian little opera, "Let's Go to Attend the Meeting of the Students' Parents," was broadly performed and received a laughing reception by the students who watched with us.

Out-of-class activities. In the schools themselves, we observed supervised and coached activities after hours (chess, painting, Ping-Pong, working in laboratories, for example). During breaks in the day before school begins, we observed vigorous and universal playground activity—there are no isolates on a Chinese playground—chiefly basketball, jump rope, and Ping-Pong.

We did not have an opportunity to observe vacation-time activities for students but we were told that there are organized games and study, apparently under the supervision of teachers, throughout vacation times. Students gather in small groups to study the works of Mao Tse-tung, to "do useful tasks," and to continue their school studies. Teachers will occasionally visit the home-based student groups during vacation to see how the work goes; they may, as well, on occasion organize visits by the students to factories, exhibits, or films.

An extracurricular enterprise that no visitor to China misses is the Shanghai Children's Palace. This grandest of all centers for children, located in what was formerly the palace of an Englishman, has been described often and we, like other visitors, were impressed by the range of activities available and, perhaps even more, by the competence of the children. Even with ten other palaces for children in Shanghai, however, the school population is almost certainly too large for all children of the city to enjoy the facilities for special study of ballet, chemistry, model building, music of all sorts, calligraphy, painting, electronics, and metalwork, and other areas. It may be that the palace serves not only to reward the industrious and the devoted but also as a subtle way of providing opportunities for further development to the academically most talented middle-school students.

Teachers and teaching

Both men and women teachers were observed in the middle schools, but the majority appear to be men at this level. Teachers ranged in age from young to middle-aged. There were both factory workers on leave to the school and retired worker-helpers in the workshops. A high proportion of the staff have been at the schools where they teach for long periods of time; many are reported to have come to the schools in the mid-1950s.

At the time of the Cultural Revolution there was a period of reeducation for many of these older teachers. The teachers from the Sian school volunteered information about their experiences during the Cultural Revolution; there was a quality of "bearing witness" about the situation as they spoke up, one by one, about their own prior ignorance about political matters. One teacher said that before the Cultural Revolution he had been an old-school intellectual who would have found it inconceivable that he would carry burdens on his shoulders or even packages in his hands. But he underwent a profound change of attitude, he reported to us, as a result of studying the works of Marx, Lenin, and Mao, of visiting factories, and of going with the students to the countryside and working alongside the peasants. The school principal explained that the school had been able to arrange for teachers to spend whole terms at a time in their reeducation. Even now, of course, teachers continue to be sent to the factories or to peasant communes for continuing reeducation.

In our briefings at middle schools, we heard again how the place of the teacher had changed over the years, particularly since the Cultural Revolution. No longer is the teacher to be seen as a member of a privileged class, inaccessible to criticism, even by students. If teachers make mistakes or "have wrong thoughts," it is the duty of their students to inform them. This two-way communication between teachers and students is intended to extend also to cooperation between them in handling behavior problems that arise in connection with schoolwork. We were told of the following instance:

A middle-school student behaved badly in class, wouldn't sit still, came late, and would on occasion actually leave school while it was still in session. The teacher would not know where he had gone and the relationship between the teacher and this student became very tense. His responsible teacher was the teacher of his English class, and when the English period came around the student always had some excuse to keep him out of class—he had a stomachache or was constipated. One day, when he left school early, the teacher followed him home. He found the student repairing a clock.

The teacher began to think it over: the more he criticized the student, the less the student attended class. With the help of the leading comrade and the student leaders (Red Guard) the teacher began to realize he needed to change his attitude. The teacher, in a meeting, criticized himself. He realized he needed to praise this student. He told the student he respected his ability to repair clocks, and said "This is something that I could learn from *you*." The student began to feel more receptive, and the teacher gave him special makeup work in English.

A note on the selection and training of teachers. Though many teachers, particularly at the kindergarten level and since the Cultural Revolution, are trained on the job, without university-level preparation, most teachers at the higher levels of the system apparently do receive formal education beyond secondary school. We were interested in how people are selected for such advanced training and how trained teachers are then selected by individual schools, and what the training itself entails. We had, therefore, a number of informal conversations with teachers and a more formal encounter with teachers of teachers from one teachers' university.

The selection of a teacher for a school is said to be made from a variety of considerations and by a variety of agents, including the Revolutionary Committee of the school, and the people in the factory or commune where the student is working. Recommendation by university teachers also play a part. The first round of the selection would appear, then, to rely on qualitative evaluations of moral, intellectual, and physical development, rather than on test documents, although we have no sure evidence on the point. It would be valuable to know how such a strongly social evaluation influences the compliance of teachers.

In at least one junior middle school we were told that since there is a teacher shortage, there is not much choice when a new teacher is needed—one simply asks the regional teachers college to send the next available person with the needed specialization. The teacher shortage reportedly stems both from the rapid expansion of educational facilities and from the fact that the teachers' colleges were closed for varying lengths of time during and following the Cultural Revolution. We interviewed several members of the psychology faculty from Shanghai's teachers' university, who explained that their university had been closed from 1966 until 1970, and had then reopened only on a limited basis, with some departments (notably psychology) beginning to enroll new students only in the fall of 1973.

When we asked how students were chosen for admission to the teachers' university, the following steps were outlined. Young people who have finished at least two years of work in the countryside, in a factory, or in the PLA are eligible to apply. Their applications must be accompanied by recommendations from members of the production brigade with which they have been working, who must certify that the applicant is willing to subordinate his own interests and serve the interests of the masses. In addition, there must be a recommendation from the local cadre in the area where the applicant has been working to testify to the applicant's political soundness. The application is then forwarded to the teachers' university. The university usually sends a team of staff members to the countryside to meet and talk with the applicants and to select those who are best qualified. They select people who are ideologically prepared to serve the people, healthy, unmarried, under the age of twenty-three, and who reach the intellectual level of a middle-school graduate. We asked how an applicant's intellectual level is determined, and were told that this is mainly accomplished through the personal interviews, though there may be more formal examinations in some instances. There was some confusion about whether the applicant had to be a senior-middle-school graduate or whether someone who had only completed the first two years of middle school could qualify. It was asserted, finally, that in exceptional circumstances a two-year applicant might be accepted, a circumstance that Chinese educators do not seem altogether pleased with.

We asked how successful the selection procedures were, whether all the students so selected proved able to handle the level of work in the teachers' university. The question seemed alien to these faculty members. They seemed to assume that any student admitted would be seen through to completion of his training. They said that of course some students learned more easily than others, so that some required more tutoring, but that it had never been necessary to drop anyone on the grounds of poor scholarship— only, once or twice, on grounds of poor health. Once admitted, the student takes a three-year course, involving course work in the various subject areas, Chinese, mathematics, history, chemistry, art, politics. The university includes a department of general psychology and a department of educational psychology. Faculty in the latter department are involved in supervising students when they go to the schools to observe teachers and how they handle classrooms. We did not discover whether any practice teaching, other than observation, was involved in the teacher training process.

Teaching methods. Students apparently have no choice within the academic curriculum, in assignments to workshops, or in the month of physical labor. When we asked, "What do students like?" we were told by cadres that it was not a question of the students' preferences; it is a question of what the society requires. From the classes we observed, it appeared that everyone in the class worked on the same assignments, an impression that is concordant with our observations in the upper primary grades. Unison oral recitation was not as commonly observed as it was at the younger ages, but it was still present in the middle schools. In addition to such uniformities, we saw variation in teaching styles, from very stereotyped, repetitive teaching of English, for example, to flexible and creative techniques for eliciting English expression from students. We observed three mathematics teachers together planning the work of their classes ("Three shoemakers may exceed a very wise person in wisdom"). They were clearly appreciative of individual variation among their students and we were struck, as well, by their enthusiasm and the liveliness of their exchange.

The work of some Chinese secondary teachers extends well beyond the teaching of their subjects in classrooms. Their hand is evident in the organization of student groups and in the training of student leaders; they organize and supervise vacation-time activities, they guide the criticism and self-criticism sessions of students, they apparently make crucial recommendations affecting the futures of their students, and they work with parents. On the last point, we were told in Sian that parents come to the middle school there for two meetings a year, that the responsible teacher visits the home of every student in his class during the year, and that, if a student is having difficulty, the teacher may make as many as seven or eight visits a month to his family. We were unable to determine how teachers were selected for these special responsibilities; we must guess that the presence of relatively larger numbers of bourgeois teachers at the upper levels puts a certain importance on maintaining political control.

Evaluation of students

The ideal expressed repeatedly in briefings and discussions at all schools was to recognize the "good" and to praise it on the spot. The injunction must be seen, however, in the context of criticism and self-criticism sessions, peers reporting on peers' behavior and urging them to do better, and close teacher-to-parent communication about the accomplishments and the weaknesses of the student. The convergence of multiple on-the-spot and around-the-clock pressures toward conformity undoubtedly comprise a powerful force for shaping behavior desired by the group and its leaders.

While we did not see any tests given or observe any record-keeping systems, tests are obviously used in China. In one middle school we were told that there are two large examinations each term, a midterm and a final, in each course, plus occasional quizzes. Teachers, of course, insist that the use of tests is quite different from what it was before the Cultural Revolution; nowadays, students are given plenty of warning in advance of a test and allowed extra time to study for it. Furthermore, teachers use open-book examinations whenever possible, since their current objective is to cultivate the student's ability to analyze problems rather than simply to memorize answers. Sometimes, they said, the teachers even announce the exam topics in advance, so that the students may consult reference books in preparing their answers. In Shanghai we were told that tests are made up by students and teachers and that students sometimes test one another.

Related to the issue of testing is the policy of moving students along with their grade, whether they are up to grade level or not. We were told that, although regular promotion was generally the practice in the primary schools, the parents (on advice of the teachers?) of a middle-school student could more readily ask that the child be kept back.

Students

Student organizations. We talked relatively little about student organizations in Chinese middle schools, but came away with the impression that the structure and function of these groups were much the same as they were in the primary-school groups. The Little Red Soldiers are succeeded in the middle schools by the Red Guard and the apparently much more selective Young Communist League, an honor organization for this age group. About half of all middle-school students are members of one or the other organization. Both are said to be primarily for discussion of political issues and for "rectification of thought" through criticism and self-criticism. Political meetings are scheduled for two or three hours each week, and sessions on current affairs are held regularly. We learned little more about Guard or League selection procedures, meeting structures, or specific forms of group sanctions.

There is some variation among student organizations from school to school. On one occasion we were told that each classroom was structured around student committees and their chairmen; there were, for example, a class leader, a study leader, a work leader, a gymnastic leader, a life-culture leader. The committee chairmen together form an executive committee for the class, and the student class leader acts as liaison between teacher and students. Students are also organized into study groups of about six to ten. These groups work both in the classroom and out of school, for cooperative study, political study, and for group criticism. Students and teachers are said to determine jointly the composition of the study groups. Finally, students also serve on the school's governing Revolutionary Committee, at least in the school we visited in Shanghai.

Although students are said to choose their leaders, the organizations all seem to be under teacher guidance and direction. We were told that an important function of the teachers is to prevent the formation of elite groups among the students, since, it was agreed, there is some tendency for the same children to appear among the leadership over time, perhaps with some changes in specific responsibility. It is also the task of the teacher to "train student leaders."

Variation among students. Nowhere are our data weaker than on assessments of individual differences or personality. Nonetheless, we observed some group and individual differences among Chinese children, of course. At the simplest level, appearance provides the first clues. Though the dull adult clothing had pretty much been adopted by the boys and the girls wore the pants and outer jackets of blue gray, we also saw bright and colorful blouses and sweaters that varied from child to child. Hair styles were still short for boys; braids and short bobs remained the styles for girls.

Differences between boys and girls. Boys and girls have the same curriculum, although in the Peking middle school, we were told that the two sexes had different areas of intellectual strength.

Girls' thought processes are slower in mathematics, physics, and chemistry but, in language, the girls are better. Under sixteen, the gap between boys and girls is not so conspicuous. [Do boys or girls generally study harder?] Girls are more diligent than boys, at least in junior middle school. At that time, the boys are more interested in playing basketball but, in senior middle school, the boys work harder on their studies.

Both boys and girls were seen in leadership positions but we do not know their relative numbers. In junior middle schools boys and girls were sometimes observed seated together, a pattern we saw less often in senior middle school. Apparently self-segregated, boys' groups and girls' groups form informally in the school yard and on the streets. Although pairs of boys and pairs of girls were often seen touching, holding hands, horsing around, we never saw adolescent boys and girls touch affectionately or hold each other. In after-school activities both boys and girls were seen engaged in workshops, in athletics, and in the arts.

Individual differences. Clearly the schools recognize and act on individual differences. In Peking, we asked whether teaching was in any way adapted to the special needs of fast students or slow students.

We admit that there is a gap and it is natural. It is also the duty of the teachers to minimize the gap; teachers must pay attention to the fastest, the slowest, and the majority—the middle level. [What do you do with the best students?] We try to bring their initiative into full play; when they have understood, and the slow ones have not yet understood, the best ones speak up. [How about the slow students?] The teacher does his best to help; after class, the teachers coach the slow students. The teacher must love the students who do not study well, not despise them. Slow students must not think the teacher is looking down on them; otherwise they will not ask the teacher questions. The students go to another student's house to help them with the concrete difficulties he has met.

In 1 or 2 percent of the students, ability is limited, but most of the students should do well. Some students, of course, may lose confidence in some subjects and say, for instance, "I'm not a person to study mathematics." We raise his courage, make him realize that he *can* do it.

There are also differences among students in how diligently they apply themselves to their work, and how fully they conform to the goals of moral behavior.

Further evidence of individualization is found in the self-criticism sessions, in the citations for achievements of individual students (for example, letters to parents or announcements on the school radio), and in the singling out of students who are not conforming. An example of the last sort was discussed by a principal.

Students sometimes show unhappiness, are quiet, do not attend classes or complete their homework. In such cases, the teacher goes to the home or sends over student cadres. For some students who are "very naughty" it is necessary to involve others from the school and neighborhood.

We did not succeed in obtaining any further information about the nature of middle-school naughtiness, but the story is, perhaps, a sufficient indication that problems of growing up and of personal and social adjustment are not altogether absent in China.

The "sending down" of urban youth

As we mentioned earlier, after either junior or senior middle school, students can be assigned to the rural and suburban countryside or to factories; the placement is according to the needs of the state "with some consideration of the student's wishes." Before the end of the last school term, workers, peasants, and revolutionary heroes come to the schools to talk about the nation's need for "educated youth"; and, we were told often, the students "are willing and eager" to serve wherever they are needed. Reportedly, if a family has only one child remaining at home he is often placed near home, and students are sometimes sent to the place where an older brother or sister has already been sent.

As we moved through China, we saw and heard the parades, with drums and flutes, that mark the departure of middle-school graduates to the countryside—for many of them, apparently a lifetime assignment. We were told that in 1972 the majority of the graduates of the Peking school went to urban or suburban factories while, in 1973, the large majority went to the countryside. Some students with badly needed skills—students of foreign languages were mentioned in particular—proceed directly to the university, and some few will come to the universities after two or three years of labor, but for the vast majority of urban Chinese students, "sending down" is evidently expected to be a permanent change in their lives.

Our hosts recognized the personal and cultural dislocation of sending down and admitted that not all youth went gladly, even that some tried to return home, but they fervently justified the procedure as a means of slowing the growth of cities, taking needed knowledge to the peasants, and guaranteeing the exposure of the educated youth to the lives of the proletariat.

A summary note

The themes that had been developing in our observation of younger children continued to play through middle school. We were surprised at the extent to which Chinese adolescents—the word "teenagers," with its usual overtones, seems inappropriate— continued to be conforming, expressive, dutiful, well organized, and apparently devoted to the values expressed by adults, and we asked ourselves the same questions we had asked earlier, about the kinds of problem solving and creative thinking being encouraged.

The students have no choices in curriculum; further, we saw no evidence of free exploration of a diversity of sources of information, of browsing in libraries, for example. Students are clearly ingesting a body of knowledge, practical knowledge. What wishes to learn more, to explore, to apply are fostered in this new generation?

The specific issue of student creativity is a difficult one about which to draw conclusions. Certainly there was more mass response and rigid regimentation in the school program in China than is typical in American schools. What evidences of creativity or resourcefulness did we see? For very talented students, there is some opportunity to invent. We have already mentioned the students who composed their own musical productions; we were also told about inventions and adaptations made by the students, with their teachers' help, in the workshops. One instance was an apparatus for holding material to be soldered, so that the worker has two free hands; another was an exhaust-fan apparatus for removing fumes from a workshop. Still another was the camera used in the production of printed circuits: the students had bought a second-hand lens (for twenty yuan, they proudly told us) and built the rest of the camera themselves. Students also had helped, presumably, in the development of a noodle-cutting machine of which they were very proud, and they were now working on a machine to crush fodder.

We saw no examples of creativity in the spheres of literature; rather, all of the literature appeared to be revolutionary stories designed to convey ideological messages. In music, though a few students were composing, our impression was again that the works consisted mainly of political songs in a kind of post-Scriabin wrapping. Except for a Rumanian selection and two American folk songs that appeared on the programs at the middle schools, and a short Beethoven selection played by a young star at the Shanghai Children's Palace, there were no signs of any foreign sources of music. From our American perspective, the regimentation and collectivity of efforts appear to produce both high uniformity and high skill in many forms of expression.

We know little about how friendships are formed or how important they may be in the life of middle-school students, although we observed a great deal of easy, pleasant hanging-on of pairs of boys and pairs of girls. Students are aware of the class backgrounds of their peers; does the information influence friendship formation? Does the inevitable break up of pairs and groups after graduation have an effect on peer relationship and peer confidences?

There are a number of conditions in the social environment of middle-school students that an American psychologist might see as relevant to self-concept, crises of values, expressed self-reliance, and generational conflicts. Questions were raised about the implications of a single strong message about cultural values and expectations, clearly prescribed and closely monitored conformity in most aspects of behavior, the lack of room for decision about a future career, and the absence of a sharp line between the private and public life of the student and his parents. It was distressing and frustrating, particularly for those of us especially interested in children of middle-school age, that we made so little headway in our attempts to register and to understand variation in personality among Chinese children.

Writing even simplified calligraphy is a demanding task. Young children in an art class and a primary-school child at a children's palace work with the traditional ink brush to form ideographs.

The sounds of Chinese (the putonghua dialect) are transcribed into phonetic pinyin and standard pronunciation of each ideograph is practiced.

7. LANGUAGE DEVELOPMENT AND EDUCATION

When Lei Feng helped someone, he never told them his name.

—From a Chinese reader

Although the delegation was charged explicitly "to discuss research on childhood learning of Chinese and foreign languages, both written and spoken," there were no opportunities to do so. It is unclear whether such research is not conducted in China, or whether the officials with whom the delegation spoke were simply unaware of it. Whatever the research situation may be, however, the consequence of our inability to talk with specialists was that our information about language development and education came largely from discussions with language teachers in the primary schools and from observations of their classroom activities. The limitations of such data are obvious; they are reported here for whatever value they may have as background for subsequent exchanges on this topic.

If further opportunities for exchange of views on language development and education should arise, we strongly recommend that the American participants be familiar with the Chinese language and system of writing, in addition to knowing psycholinguistic research. Lacking such a combination of competencies, the present delegation spent considerable time discovering basic facts about Chinese that should have been known in advance. And the need to rely on interpreters added further limitations to the reliability of the information we were able to obtain.

Since the reader may also be unfamiliar with Chinese, some of the more important facts will be summarized here, to provide a basis for understanding educational practices. Readers familiar with Chinese may wish to skip the following section and go directly to the report of our conversations and observations.

About the Chinese language

The most important point for a speaker of Indo-European languages to keep in mind when approaching Chinese is the high frequency of homophones (words like "colonel" and "kernel" that have the same sound, but different meanings). The Peking dialect has 405 syllables; a comparable figure for English is not known, but there must be at least ten times as many. The Peking dialect increases its stock of syllables by distinguishing four tones. For example, *wān* (level tone) means "to bend," *wán* (rising tone) means "to finish," *wǎn* (falling, then rising tone) means "late," and *wàn* (falling tone) means "ten thousand."

Chinese words are not all monosyllables; disyllables are very frequent in the vernacular. The polysyllabic words are, however, with few exceptions, compounded of syllables that can occur in their own right as morphemes (the smallest meaningful units of a language); *da-xiang-mao* ("big-bear-cat"), for example, is the name for panda. That is to say, Chinese is an analytic, not an inflected language; almost every syllable can be used as a free form (unlike such bound forms in English as *dis-, -ly, -er, -ed*). Nearly every morpheme is a single syllable and, since there are far more than 1,620 smallest meaningful units, most syllables must represent several different morphemes. The consequence is a high degree of homophony that can only be disambiguated by the context of use.

Chinese script represents the morphemes of spoken Chinese, one character per syllable. Different homophones are represented by different characters, so that the potential homophonic ambiguities of the spoken language are eliminated in the written language. On the printed page, however, no word boundaries are apparent; each Chinese character can be either a word in its own right or part of a polysyllabic word (just as phrase boundaries are not apparent in printed English). It proved difficult to ask how segmentation is learned; teachers responded with the same puzzlement an American teacher might feel if asked to explain how children are taught to recognize idioms like "once upon a time" as semantic units.

The variety of Chinese dialects poses a serious problem for modern China. Speakers of the Canton or Shanghai dialects, for example, cannot understand one another. Since Chinese characters are not phonemic, however, educated Chinese speaking different dialects have been able to communicate in writing; the fact that they would make different vocal sounds when they saw the same characters does not prevent the characters from having the same meanings for everyone. Because this channel is important for national unity, China could not presently abandon the characters in favor of alphabetic writing even if it wished to. Yet there is a clear need for more linguistic uniformity than Chinese script provides.

Attempts to impose a national language have a complex history. The Chinese Republic in 1912 chose Mandarin, the dialect of Chinese spoken by officials, as the national language, but it was not until 1949 that the People's Republic of China seriously undertook to teach Mandarin (also called *putonghua,* "common speech") to everyone. Today, children in Canton or Shanghai are taught by the schools to speak, read, and write a dialect of Chinese very different from the dialects they learn at home. They also learn a much simplified set of written characters; the reduction in number of strokes in many characters probably made literacy more generally available. This teaching is said to be successful with every normal child, though we were unable to determine to what degree and with what variability. Such success is remarkable in view of our American experience, where, with far less linguistic diversity, many children fail to acquire basic literacy skills in our schools.

To teach students a new way of speaking, it has been necessary to introduce some way to indicate the correct sounds of putonghua. For this purpose, the Chinese officially adopted the Roman alphabet in 1956, defining it in terms of Peking phonology. This alphabetic form of writing, called *pinyin,* may eventually replace character writing, but not until putonghua is truly the common speech of everyone. For the present and for the indefinite future, writing will be done with characters and pinyin will be primarily an aid in teaching Peking pronunciations.

These massive changes in the speech habits of the Chinese people are an important part of the continuing revolution prescribed for modern China by Chairman Mao. To carry them out, universal education through primary school is essential.

First language learning

No one with whom we spoke knew of any systematic observations of first-language learning by Chinese children, nor did they express interest in hearing of such studies in other countries. This situation was disappointing; given the simple and flexible nature of Chinese syntax, comparative studies would be of considerable interest if they were available.

Most Chinese children spend their first three years outside the preschools, and many do not enter the system until the age of six or seven. By this age, of course, they will have become relatively competent users of whatever dialect is spoken in their homes. Those who attend kindergarten between the ages of three and six may encounter teachers who use only putonghua, but that is by no means universal; we heard the Canton dialect in Canton kindergartens, the Sian dialect in Sian kindergartens, and the Shanghai dialect in Shanghai kindergartens. If teaching putonghua in every kindergarten is an eventual goal, it is still far from being achieved.

Teaching putonghua. Kindergarten children have some initial exposure to important characters, but as in American schools, the serious teaching of reading and writing begins in the first grade. For children in and around Peking, the skills to be mastered are comparable, given the difference in orthography, to those we try to teach most children in the United States. But for the majority of Chinese children (and, one may be suspect, for some of their teachers), the task is more difficult, since they must learn at the same time to speak a new dialect, one that is usually far less similar to their first than, say, the black English vernacular is to standard English. The task cannot be likened to teaching an American child French or German in the first grade, because Chinese grammar is common to all the dialects, but the amount of new phonological and lexical knowledge to be mastered is considerable.

American experience has been that approximately 1,600 contact hours are required for an adult to gain conversational fluency in a foreign language. Lacking any better estimate, therefore, we might expect that a child given 20 contact hours a week for forty weeks a year would, after two years, be a competent user of putonghua. And since putonghua is not really a different language, one can believe that, as we were told, most children can understand it in less than a year, though some rural children are not truly fluent speakers until the fifth or sixth grade. Clearly, there are many other factors (motivation, local pride, fluency of teachers in putonghua) that will influence rate of acquisition.

In first grade teaching of pinyin begins. In Peking we were told that learning the alphabet takes three weeks, with another week and a half for consolidation. Not unexpectedly, learning pinyin takes somewhat longer when the child is unfamiliar with putonghua; in Sian we were told that it takes five weeks, at a rural commune in Shensi province six weeks, and in Shanghai five weeks. In any case, within just a few weeks the children are said to master the letter–phoneme correspondences of pinyin. Since many American children fail to master the letter–phoneme correspondences of English after three years, such an achievement is impressive evidence for the advantages of a phonetically regular alphabet, the effectiveness of Chinese teaching methods, or the uniform attentiveness and motivation of the Chinese child. Or all three.

We were told that all schools begin reading instruction with pinyin. The method of teaching it, however, may differ from district to district. In Peking, for example, we were told that the phonemic values of the alphabetic symbols were taught before any Chinese characters were introduced. In a Sian school, pinyin was introduced more gradually: a teacher there said that they begin with simple Chinese characters and teach, for each character, the pinyin representation of its putonghua pronunciation, the form of the character and how to write it, and its meaning, in that order. This three-fold association of sound, form, and meaning was emphasized by several teachers. Unfortunately, our visit occurred after this initial instruction in pinyin had ended, so we were unable to observe the teaching methods employed.

Questions about difficulties in putting the phonemes together to form syllables, a process usually called *blending* in the United States, were well understood. We were told that initially blending is a problem for most children; teachers described various techniques, all of which would be familiar to reading teachers in America, that they use to help children over this difficulty. Even with these aids, some children have great trouble with blending; one teacher estimated that there would be two or three in every class of fifty students. But they claimed that all children mastered it eventually. It should be noted, however, that a child who does not master pinyin is not seriously handicapped as long as he is able to learn the pronunciation of Chinese characters directly.

Once pinyin is mastered, the work of learning characters begins in earnest. New characters are introduced at a rate of 20 to 25 per week. The total number of characters a graduate of primary school is expected to know varies from school to school; in a rural school we were told 2,000, in one urban school 3,500, and other schools gave numbers falling within this range. It has been asserted that 2,000 characters are required for functional literacy, i.e., to read newspapers, public documents, and so on. However, Chinese newspapers are now permitted to use up to 3,000 characters and some primary-school graduates may not be literate in a fully functional way. Technological sidelight: the character typewriters we saw contained fewer than 2,000 characters but had replaceable units.

The order in which characters are introduced is determined by the textbooks prepared by the educational committees of the districts or cities. Since the Cultural Revolution these readers have been repeatedly revised to strengthen their ideological message, but the order in which characters are introduced was said to be determined on other grounds; simplicity of the character's form, frequency of use, and relevance to the child's life. The order of introduction may vary according to the province; since there is little mobility of families from one province to another, differences of this sort would pose no serious problems.

When a new character is introduced it is always accompanied—on flashcards, on the blackboard, in the text—by the pinyin spelling of its pronunciation. After a child has formed the connection between a character and its pronunciation, the form of the character is analyzed. Most characters have two parts. One part belongs to a set of radicals that are used to arrange the characters in an order for dictionaries, catalogs, and so on; the second part sometimes, but not always, suggests its pronunciation—i.e., was originally borrowed from a homophone. Children are expected to learn about 120 of the important radicals in the first two grades.

It is also necessary to learn the order of drawing the strokes in each character. In cursive writing the pen may not always be lifted between strokes, in which case the wrong order produces a meaningless pattern. Each of the basic strokes has a name, and the children recite the stroke names as they draw them, much as an American child might say "dee oh tee" as he wrote "dot." It is an impressive sight when a class of forty or fifty children respond to a flashcard by chanting in unison, "heng heng shu heng dian," while waving their arms with pointed fingers to indicate the appropriate strokes.

In Chinese language classes we saw a good deal of chanting in unison. The use of this traditional method of instruction in China has reportedly been reduced since 1949, but we were told that it is still an effective method of teaching languages, helping students to improve their sound articulation, though less appropriate for mathematical and scientific subjects.

Shouting in unison, shouting the same thing repeatedly in unison, shouting in unison to echo the teacher, and listening to other students shouting are all components of the language learning process. It is not enough to mumble the formulas being memorized; every student must sing them out, loud and clear. The noise so generated seems merely to advertise to other classes how earnestly one's own class is working. It also, of course, confirms in yet another mode the emphasis on group cooperation and the low public valuation of individual competition.

Since vigorous repetition of each formula seems to be the method of learning each new character, repeated questions were asked about the teaching of rules and general principles. For example, there are seven rules for determining the order of strokes in a character. When asked how these rules were taught, one teacher replied that the children first learned a group of characters that illustrated the rule, and only after that did the teacher point out to them the rule that governed stroke order in all those characters.

The third aspect of the character to be taught is its meaning. This requires less drill for children who already speak the Peking dialect. For those who do not, a variety of teaching procedures are used, e.g., identifying pictures of the referent, or using words in the context of a sentence. In more advanced classes considerable time may be spent reciting combinations of a new character with other characters in words or idioms.

When we asked whether every child who graduated from primary school was able to read and write, the answer was affirmative, although the teachers were uncertain of what we meant by "able to read and write." They admitted to variability among children (reported as well by other observers), but it was clear that the variability they testified to was substantially smaller than would be found in the United States. Unfortunately, however, quantitative data on this point were not available and are, of course, critical in assessing the success of the programs for language education.

Rules of grammar are not taught until the third or, more often, fourth grade. At that time children are taught to name the major syntactic categories or "parts of speech" and to recognize the difference between the subject and the predicate of a sentence. For example, predicates like "work for the collective" or "help each other" will be written on the board in characters, and children will be asked to provide appropriate subjects to fill the blanks.

In a more advanced language class a period may be spent reading and analyzing a short text. The title of the text may be written on the blackboard before the students arrive; it may deal with the importance of hydroelectric power, or how to recognize minerals in rocks, or some other practical topic, usually related to a quotation from Chairman Mao. The teacher may read a sentence aloud, in putonghua, then the class chants it in unison; the teacher reads the next sentence, and the class chants that one; and so on through the text. Then the teacher may put up a prepared slate on the chalk tray; it will usually present six new characters, whose pronunciation is written above them in pinyin, and the teacher will discuss them. Then the children will recite these aloud in unison many times as the teacher points to them in haphazard order. Then a student may read the text aloud as the class follows it in their readers. The class again reads the text, now aloud in unison. The teacher may next analyze the argument into its main points in outline form, the class repeating these points in unison after they are written on the board. Or the teacher may test comprehension by asking questions that must be answered by reading an appropriate sentence from the text. Finally, the remaining time may be spent by the students writing and rewriting the new characters in their copy books. The same text may be read again the next day, with six other characters chosen for drill. The students accept this kind of drill docilely and, as far as we could tell, in good humor. And they learn to read and write putonghua.

Second-language learning

Our opportunities for observing the teaching of foreign languages were severely limited. The classes we did see, however, suggested that the methods used to teach English or Russian were similar to those used to teach putonghua. Highly repetitive drills chanted in unison were used. Although the instructors were not uniformly good models for the students to imitate, the method of teaching seemed to be effective in learning English phonology.

According to two English teachers interviewed in Shanghai, they begin by teaching the English alphabet: "aye, bee, see, . . . " The real drill on English begins with the memorization of phrases that can occur in simple dialogue: "What is your name?" "Where do you study?" "How old are you?" "Are you a Red Guard?" The children learn to make simple answers in English, but we once observed a child respond to one question with an answer appropriate to another. For supplementary work, some students memorize ideological verses in English.

Students are expected to learn about twenty new words, one lesson in the text, each week; after four years of studying English in middle school they are expected to know how to use 1,500–2,000 words.

We were unable to determine how grammar was taught, other than by memorizing sentences that illustrate grammatical regularities. Nor were we able to determine how the teacher evaluated a student's comprehension. The program seemed geared to producing students who could hold simple conversations with foreigners.

kindergarten teacher tells a story ("The Cock Crows at Midnight") with the help of
otographs of puppets. Along the wall under the pictures are the ever-present
ashcloths that are used to assure clean hands and faces.

he children we saw ate well and skillfully everything set before them. Chopsticks
e used by the age of three.

Chinese children practice the four eye exercises illustrated on the chalkboard. The exercises, meant to prevent myopia, occupy them for twenty minutes of every school day of every school year.

8. HEALTH AND NUTRITIONAL FACTORS

In health care, put the stress on prevention. In medical and health work, put the stress in rural areas.

—Mao Tse-tung, 1947

The delegation's investigation of health care for children in China was special in several ways. Unlike child development, the character of Chinese medical care had already been widely reported by American visitors; though unlike some earlier delegations, our pediatric observer came to China with a rich experience of medicine in developing countries. And while all the members of our delegation, with their varied backgrounds, studied Chinese children in settings of school and family, we depended on a single energetic pediatrician to observe medical practice.[1] For these reasons, our notes on health care differ somewhat from earlier chapters; the medical report is more explicitly comparative and it is more often quantitative. It shares with the rest of the report an emphasis on what we saw and measured ourselves.

Our hosts in China let us see a great variety of health-care facilities, in many different settings—urban neighborhoods, factories, and rural communes—although our sample was, as usual, highly selective, extremely small, and unrepresentative of remote rural areas. We had little time, and, worse, our translators were usually unfamiliar with either Chinese or Western medical terminology. Nonetheless, special arrangements were made for Dr. Wray to visit the Children's Hospital and the Capital Hospital in

1. Only a brief summary of Dr. Wray's observations appears in the present report; he has prepared a fuller account for *Pediatrics* 55 (1974): 539–50, 723–34.

Peking and for interviews with the specialist on newborns and with
several obstetrician-gynecologists from the International Peace
Infant and Maternity Hospital in Shanghai.

Housing and sanitation

Nowhere in China did we see the contrasts so striking in other
developing countries, between small, affluent elites living in comfortable luxury and poverty-stricken masses living in crowded
squatter slums. The homes and apartments we saw, both in urban
and rural areas, were small, somewhat crowded, and rather
sparsely furnished. They were, however, invariably neat and
reasonably clean. Water is said to be potable everywhere, although the Little Red Soldiers are told not to drink unboiled water. We saw no open sewers or garbage-infested streets; there are
almost no flies. There was remarkably little trash to be seen
anywhere, partly because the standard and style of living simply
does not produce a great deal of waste and whatever can possibly
be used or reused is.

Food

It can only be said that, as special foreign guests in homes in
rural communes on two occasions, we were offered far more of a
healthy variety of foods than we could possibly consume, which
was undoubtedly a more accurate reflection of hospitality than of
daily diet. But repeated questioning in the homes, schools, and
health centers we visited brought responses indicating that the
Chinese diet is nowadays generally adequate, both in quantity and
quality.

The ideology of health care

Throughout our visit in China, we heard people attribute
achievements to "following the mass line of Chairman Mao"—
achievements including increases in factory outputs, irrigation

systems, dams, new crops, better crop yields, and a host of other things. How this works in the health field was brought home vividly in an interview with Dr. Lin Ch'iao-chih, chairman of Obstetrics and Gynecology at the Capital Hospital in Peking. Dr. Lin, gracious and vivacious, graduated from Peking Union Medical College in 1929. When she was asked about China's most impressive health-care change, she replied, "Flies!"

> You can't imagine how utterly awful the flies were in Peking in the old days! I remember very well how one day [many years ago, Dr. John Grant of the Rockefeller Foundation] came to class and discussed with us a very careful plan to control the flies in Peking. He had calculated everything—the insecticides needed, the manpower, the cost. But then he said to us, 'So you see, the control of flies is technically possible, but it can't happen: the government won't provide the money and the public won't cooperate!' He was right at the time, of course, but after Liberation it was not too difficult at all. We just followed the mass line of Chairman Mao. First we taught the people how important it is to control the flies to stop the spread of disease. After everyone understood, they all helped clean up the streets, and then we gave the grandmothers and children fly swatters, and they all went to work. We had contests—people collected dead flies in bottles to see which neighborhood could kill the most! Soon there were no more flies! It didn't take long and it cost very little. Have you seen any flies in Peking?

Health care in general

Decentralization. One of the truly striking things about the health care system in China is its degree of decentralization. Reportedly there are fewer than two hundred people in the health bureaucracy in Peking, although the future became uncertain when the central health bureaucracy was reestablished early in 1975. A given health policy is said to be decided upon high in the system, passed along with detailed but general instructions, and then assigned to the appropriate local unit, which figures out how to carry it out in its particular setting. There was considerable variation in the details of staffing patterns from place to place, for example, even within our limited range, but it appeared, in the settings we observed, that the same basic array of health care services was being provided responsibly and capably.

Number of health workers. Estimates of the number of Western-style physicians in China before 1949 vary from ten to forty thousand; in addition there were approximately five hundred thousand practitioners of traditional Chinese medicine. It is reported that by 1966 the number of doctors of Western medicine had increased to around one hundred and sixty thousand. Meantime, traditional practitioners had been incorporated into the health care system and, to some extent at least, taught certain Western concepts, while Western-style doctors were learning acupuncture. And special paramedical personnel have been trained, the best known of which are the "barefoot doctors." The result of these efforts, although we cannot attest to the typicality of our observations, seems to be an abundance of personnel: a production-brigade health center serving six to ten production teams (a population of two or three thousand) had two or three part-time barefoot doctors (who have, at most, the rough equivalent of a junior-middle-school education); a kindergarten with an enrollment of several hundred children had a full-time health staff of three, including one doctor.

Training of health personnel. The various categories of health personnel have apparently had a bewildering variety of training, impossible to describe in detail. The following kinds of general policies have been sifted out from the many briefings we were given.

For people in all categories the stress in training is said to be on learning through practice; formal, didactic training is kept to a minimum.

The training, whether didactic or on-the-job, is provided as close to the home base as possible. In the case of the barefoot doctors, the middle-level people in the health-care system, training is provided by qualified physicians who go to the locality of the barefoot doctors and provide their training in the place in which they are expected to work. Production-team or neighborhood health workers are trained in local health centers.

Continuing education is reportedly provided both in on-the-job guidance and in weekly or biweekly meetings.

Everyone interviewed, at whatever level in the system, seemed to have been trained adequately for functioning at his or her particular level; they could define the problems they were expected to handle, knew what to do about them, and where to refer problems beyond their own abilities.

Social distance. How well people understand health care instructions, and carry them out, is in many cultures a function of the social distance between them and the person providing the care. In China the person delivering primary care and responsible for preventive services or health education is often a fellow worker who has had the minimum essential training. At the next level, the barefoot doctor is also supposed to be from the community he serves. Physicians and nurses have been extensively "reeducated" through long assignments in rural areas, during which they provide medical care, train barefoot doctors, participate in productive labor, and "learn from the peasants." In conversations with physicians, we were told that their reeducation in the country had brought them "closer to the people."

Accessibility. The distance to the nearest health care facility seems, in most countries, to determine the promptness with which care is sought and whether or not preventive services are utilized. One of the most impressive features of the Chinese health care system we heard about is its extension to the neighborhood level. To be sure, our sample of settings was small and selected, but if we measure accessibility by it a Chinese clearly does not have to travel far—sometimes no more than a few hundred yards—to the nearest available health care.

Back-up facilities. The adequacy of a health-care system also depends, to a very large extent, on the availability of more sophisticated facilities and personnel with better training "up the line," and, no less important, a communication and transportation system adequate to make use of these facilities possible when necessary. Our observations, and those of others, suggest that the system in China today is at least minimally adequate in this respect. The peripheral units in the system were very simply equipped, with thermometers, stethoscopes, a variety of modern drugs and traditional Chinese medicines, health education and family planning posters, and sometimes acupuncture needles. At each level higher, the facilities were somewhat larger, better staffed, and more thoroughly equipped, so that at commune hospitals, for example, we saw simple X-ray units, laboratories for blood, urine, and stool examinations, simply but adequately equipped surgical suites, oxygen tents, intravenous feeding apparatus (which we observed being used) and, in some such hospitals, facilities for preparing intravenous fluids and manufacturing traditional herb medicines.

Cost. Rising costs of medical care are a serious obstacle to the prompt procurement of care in some Western countries, as well as in all developing countries. We were given the impression that the problem is less serious in China. As with so many other things we saw, there is a confusing variety of methods of financing health care and we did not have time to explore details or opportunity to verify what we were told and what we guessed.

Some workers, we were told, are covered by health insurance. Others pay annual fees, as well as token fees for each service received. These are low by Western standards and seem to be within the means of all Chinese. They are supplemented by substantial subsidies provided, before wages are paid, out of the profits of the major production units—large factories and communes—which are responsible for the overall health care of the populations in their units. We do not know what priority is given health care when there are low or no profits, nor do we know how many Chinese are covered in this way. Further subsidies are provided out of taxes collected at the county or province level. The costs of family-planning services and supplies come from these sources.

Health workers in rural communes are reported to accumulate work points just as do other workers, and are paid, like their fellows, on the basis of these points.

The widespread utilization of both acupuncture and the traditional Chinese herb medicines may be an important factor in keeping costs low.

Ideology, patriotism, and education. As we have often noted, there is a vast social apparatus for transmitting Mao Tse-tung's thoughts, both in schools and neighborhoods, and this apparatus can be used as an adjunct to health care. Such was the case, for example, in the massive campaigns to control "the four pests" (sparrows, rats, flies, and mosquitoes) in the 1950s, and, presently, with regard to family planning. What this means, for practical purposes, is that for certain health-related policies, noncompliance is unpatriotic. We were told, for example, that the ideas that "many children bring happiness" and "sons are necessary for security in old age" are now considered "feudal." Persuasion, as well as medicine, is part of health care in China.

Family size and "birth planning"

There is almost complete unanimity in the reports of recent visitors to China that progress in limiting births is being made, and we too were told about birth rates ranging from 4 to 20 per 1,000 population. Perhaps the most interesting data obtained during our visit were provided by the staff of the Tsao-yang "Street Hospital," an urban health center providing out-patient care and preventive services to a New Workers' Quarters' population of approximately 70,000 in Shanghai. Like other data reported from China, these come from a relatively small urban population and are of undetermined reliability. They may be of interest, however, because comparable data, showing birth rate trends over time in China, have not often been reported. In the early 1960s, birth rates ranged between 33 and 24 per 1,000; then an altogether remarkable drop occurred between 1963 and 1964, when the rates fell from 21 to 11 births per 1,000. The rate has since continued to fall, with some variations, to the incredibly low level of 5.28 in 1972. There were reported to be only 360 births in the district in 1972, and we were told that there were no deaths of newborns and no prematures. It is unfortunate, given these remarkable data, that we do not know the age distribution of the quarters' population. Our intrepretations would vary, of course, if it turned out that, because it is an old neighborhood, a significant part of the drop in birth rate represented the aging of a relatively stable population, now largely past the childbearing period.

The pattern of health-care delivery can be illustrated, perhaps, by a brief description of that in the Tsao-yang New Workers' Quarters. First occupied in 1952, largely by illiterate factory workers or laborers, the quarters consist of two- to five-story buildings with two- or three-room flats, all with running water, gas, electricity, and "sanitary equipment," in contrast to "the huts and garrets" where we were told the population lived before. Health-care and family-planning services (which the Chinese call "birth planning") are provided in the street hospital (backed up by the 500-bed Pu-to Central Hospital which also serves eight other districts with a total population of six hundred thousand), and twelve neighborhood health posts, called "cooperative medical protective–curative stations." The health-center staff reportedly includes thirteen doctors, both Western and traditional, twenty-four nurses, nine technicians, and eighteen caretakers. Each neighborhood health station is reportedly staffed by one nurse from the street hospital and four or five neighborhood health workers. For the most part, these are said to be older, literate, married women who have received three months of formal training followed by on-the-job training provided on a continuing basis by the nurse from the hospital.

Each neighborhood served by the health station has a Committee on Planned Birth Work responsible for "education and motivation" in family planning. We were told elsewhere that earlier all physicians and other health workers had to participate in such activities, but now "everyone has the idea" and the health workers merely provide the services, leaving motivation to the committees. Neighborhood health workers are to provide information, advice, and oral contraceptives. The health center reportedly provides IUD insertions, and abortions in the case of contraceptive failure. Sterilization procedures are carried out at the district hospital. All of these services are said to be free of charge.

The Yang-pu New Workers' Quarters, which our delegation also visited, is similar to Tsao-yang in all respects, but has a smaller population. We were told that there were in 1972 a total of 219 births, with 2 deaths of newborns and four infants weighing less than 2,500 grams at birth. The birth rate in this district would thus be approximately 5 per 1,000. Between January and September of 1973, there were said to be a total of 92 births, with no newborn or infant deaths, and 90 deaths in adults—giving a birthrate below 3 per 1,000 and a net population gain of 2 among forty-four thousand people! Rates for previous years were not available for this district and, of course, no data can be accurately interpreted without knowing something about the age structure and migration patterns of the population.

Birth rates for all of Shanghai were reported by Drs. Chang, Cheng, and Fan of the Shanghai International Peace Maternity Hospital. Shanghai has a total population of more than ten million, of which approximately six million live in the city and over four million live in the surrounding countryside in agricultural communes. In 1972 the average birth rate in the suburban communes was said by our hosts to be 15.9 per 1,000, and slightly over 6 per 1,000 in the city itself. Of course, we cannot assess the impact on birthrates of the fact that at least one million young people have been sent from Shanghai to the countryside since 1968.

Everywhere we visited, it was acknowledged that birth rates reported in Shanghai are the lowest in the country. In Peking, we were told that the 1972 birth rate for the municipality was approximately 14 per 1,000, and this was invariably compared with the lower rate in Shanghai. The low birth rates reported for Peking and Shanghai (none were obtained for Canton or Sian) were everywhere praised and given strong social support. Teachers in the various schools we visited, for example, were unanimous and uniform in their comments regarding family size—"two children are enough"; "we don't need to have sons." When, in two different factories, we asked whether maternity benefits were decreased after the second child we were assured that this is not the practice, but that, in fact, very few employees are now giving birth to third children.

Estimates of birth rates given to us for rural areas near cities varied around the figure of 20 per 1,000. There was, among our informants, universal acknowledgment of wide variation and, again, of the fact that the birth rate deep in the country is higher than that of cities or suburbs. The birth-planning services provided in the countryside are said to be basically similar to those in the cities and the network, we were told, is expanding. Oral and other contraceptives, IUDs, and abortions are available at brigade health centers, and sterilizations are performed in the commune hospitals. Oral contraceptives may also sometimes be distributed at the level of the production team by barefoot doctors. Dr. Lin Ch'iao-chih, who, like some other urban-based Chinese physicians, had spent many months working in rural areas, provided some interesting insights. Over half of all barefoot doctors are women, she said, and in most production brigades a woman barefoot doctor is designated "maternity specialist" and is being taught, more and more often, to insert IUDs and perform abortions using a simple suction system. When asked about complications—hemorrhage, uterine rupture, or infection—following such procedures performed by these women Dr. Lin replied that such occurrences are extremely rare and, if anything, less frequent than they are when physicians perform the same procedures. Why? "Doctors tend to be a bit casual about such things; barefoot doctors take them more seriously!" She also reported that although men in rural China are reluctant to submit to vasectomies, some rural production brigades have outstandingly high vasectomy rates. "It all depends on the spirit of the people."

In addition to the widespread availability of birth-planning services, there are reported to be in rural areas, as in the cities, community-based women's groups responsible for monitoring and motivation. Of the rural communes we visited, the lowest birth rate was reported in the most remote—in rural Shensi— where the birth rate for 1972 was reported as a little over 10 per 1,000. The barefoot doctor there told us that he attends a monthly meeting attended by approximately 100 barefoot doctors from other production brigades in their county and, on the basis of reports he has heard there, the rate in his brigade is about average for the county. In a rural commune not far from Canton, we were told that the birth rate was 28 per 1,000 in 1966 and had fallen to 20 per 1,000 in 1972; at the July First People's Commune outside Shanghai, the birth rate for 1972 was reported as 12 per 1,000. Research is clearly needed on the geographic and demographic variation in both Chinese goals and Chinese achievements in population control.

The birth rates reported here and by other visitors to China are so low that they strain credulity. Visitors, obviously, have no way to check the validity of figures provided them. Moreover, Shanghai is reported to be more advanced in the development of birth-control programs than any other city in China. There was, however, a congruence between the birth-rate data we were given and what we were told about those socioeconomic factors that are associated with lowered birth rates in other countries—later age of marriage, a higher proportion of women in the work force, increasing literacy, concern for child health, availability of safe abortion, sufficient contraceptive information and materials, and a forceful system of ideological support against premarital pregnancies and large families. Assuming all of these circumstances for China, the rates reported are still remarkably low, but more believable.

Maternal factors in early childhood development

Maternal health. The statistically average Chinese woman lives on a commune and is an active worker. For much of each year she is therefore called upon to perform the vigorous physical labor involved in planting and harvesting crops. A large majority of the women who live in cities are also employed, many of them in factories, and are also physically active. Thus, the proportion of women, especially those in their twenties and early thirties, who lead sedentary, inactive lives is extremely small and most women appear to be in excellent physical condition.

Maternal age and marital status. There has been a steady campaign in China to delay the age at marriage. The regime's target is twenty-five for women and twenty-seven for men. We were told that the target has been reached in cities but that in the countryside the average age of marriage for women is still well under twenty-five. Of course, large-scale data are simply unavailable to foreigners, and some observers report that the target ages for marriage are more long-term goals than achievements. We were also told that premarital pregnancy "is not zero, but it's very rare and when it happens, it is taken very seriously." Thus the Chinese hope is that complications for the mother or the newborn associated with either early or illegitimate pregnancies are being effectively combatted.

Maternal nutrition. Numerous reports of life in traditional China suggest that malnutrition—with its potential for affecting the tissues of pregnant women and their babies—was probably extremely common. Today, at least in the places we visited, the danger is apparently markedly reduced. Both the quantity and variety of foods available in China has increased significantly and the improvement seems to be reflected in better maternal diets.

From repeated questioning, it appeared that education about diet during pregnancy consisted primarily of encouraging women to eat the "good foods" they were, perhaps, already disposed to eat. When Dr. Lin Ch'iao-chih was asked whether there were any problems posed by traditional dietary customs during pregnancy, she reported that occasionally it was necessary to caution women about eating too many eggs because of the widespread idea that eggs are "good for you" during pregnancy. She also asserted that anemia during pregnancy, formerly commonplace, is now rare, as is toxemia, and reported that average weight gain during pregnancy is over twenty pounds.

Smoking. It seems worth noting that although smoking is a widespread habit among men in China, we were told and we observed that it is uncommon among women, especially those of childbearing age. Whatever impairment of fetal growth might be expected as a result of maternal smoking during pregnancy is therefore avoided in all but a small fraction of the population.

Antenatal care. The many factors mentioned previously that seem to make health care in China generally accessible geographically, economically, and socially must be kept in mind in considering antenatal care in China. Together with the various neighborhood women's organizations, these factors may make it difficult for a pregnant woman to escape notice; we were told that essentially all women, both in cities and in the countryside, receive antenatal care.

The emphasis, as our informants in many places reiterated, is on identifying "high-risk" women—those who are more likely than others to have some sort of complication at the time of delivery—so that proper care can be provided for such complications as may arise. In rural areas, this means sending certain expectant mothers to the commune hospital; other rural women are usually delivered by the barefoot-doctor "maternity specialists" in brigade medical stations or midwives at home. In the cities, mothers who may have problems are sent to specialized maternity hospitals or district general hospitals. Antenatal care is otherwise routine; there are said to be monthly visits during early and midpregnancy, and at more frequent intervals after the eighth month in the cities; we have no testimony about rural practice. Advice is reportedly provided regarding diet during pregnancy and for the baby to come; blood pressure and urine are checked regularly to detect toxemia of pregnancy, which is said to be less frequent than formerly.

Obstetrical care. Almost every birth in China is said to be attended by trained personnel—prepared midwives or barefoot doctors—whether in the city or in the countryside, and, as noted above, those cases in which complications are expected are routinely referred to hospitals. Several features of the care provided are important to note. The overwhelming majority of deliveries are apparently spontaneous; forceps are, according to report, hardly ever used; vacum extraction is used only in unusual circumstances in larger hospitals. Acupuncture anesthesia is increasingly used. The use of sedatives or anesthetics of any sort, which might affect the fetus, is said to be rare. Caesarean sections, when indicated, are performed under epidural blocks or with acupuncture anesthesia. At the International Peace Maternity Hospital in Shanghai, the Caesarean rate is reportedly under 4 percent; at the Capital Hospital in Peking, it was reported to vary from 4 to 6 percent, becoming higher in recent years, we were told, because Caesareans are more frequently performed if a tubectomy is desired anyway. Both of these hospitals, it might be noted, deliver women already identified as high-risk cases. Unfortunately, completely satisfactory data on labor and delivery are lacking, but the information available to us suggests the following tentative conclusions.

Among 4,400 deliveries at the International Peace Hospital in Shanghai during 1972 there were reported to be twenty-four deaths of newborns, giving a rate of approximately 5.5 per 1,000 live births. Prematurity was the cause of seven of these deaths, hyaline membrane disease and congenital cardiac malformations four each, and other malformations and intrauterine anoxia with associated intracranial hemorrhage caused the rest. No comparable data were obtained elsewhere.

The rate of premature births, as evidenced by birth weights below 2,500 grams, is apparently low. At the International Peace Hospital again, of all babies delivered between 1958 and 1970, only 5 percent were reported as premature; in 1972, the figure was 4.3 percent. Elsewhere during our visit, a variety of anecdotal information by obstetricians and midwives alike conveyed one message: babies weighing less than 2,500 grams at birth are unusual.

With regard to birth weights generally we collected almost no data. In Shanghai, the mean birth weight for males was reported to be 3,150 grams, for females, 3,100. Elsewhere, estimates consistently over 3,000 grams were provided. In rural Shensi the figure given was 3,500 grams.

Health care of children

We concluded, early in our visit, that there is not one pattern of health care for infants and children carried out everywhere. There is great variation from one health-care facility to another and in the types of health personnel who staff such facilities. However, certain basic activities seemed to be present everywhere we went.

Well-child supervision. Infants are seen, examined, and weighed and measured at regular intervals in most places visited, with considerable variation in the schedule from place to place. On these visits, mothers are given dietary advice and immunizations are provided. These visits may be carried out at health centers or, in some cases, the health personnel visit the mother and infant at home. Health and nutrition education are said to be provided to small groups of mothers, and community women's organizations are also used as a channel for such education. It was also mentioned in several places that neighborhood groups are used, especially to educate grandmothers in modern concepts of child care and nutrition. This is of obvious importance since in many families grandmothers are responsible for children when the mother is at work, and in others they may be inclined to interfere.

Immunizations. A very complete array of immunizations is reportedly provided to the overwhelming majority of infants and young children in China. The general pattern is to provide innoculation against tuberculosis at birth, Type I oral polio vaccine in the second month, combined Type II and III in the third month. The DPT (diptheria, pertussis, tetanus) series is begun at three months, and continued at monthly intervals for a total of three doses. Smallpox vaccination is carried out at the seventh month and measles vaccine is given at the eighth month. Booster doses of all these vaccines are said to be provided at appropriate intervals. Children in nursery schools and kindergartens are provided a vaccine against epidemic meningitis twice a year after the first year of life, and are vaccinated against encephalitis B in May or June of each year.

These immunizations are said to be provided in the production-team health stations in rural areas and in the neighborhood co-operative medical protective-curative stations in urban areas. An immunization record is kept for each child and it is apparently checked periodically to be sure that "his shots are up-to-date." Whenever it is necessary, as indicated by the record, health personnel go directly to homes to provide the immunizations there. In many districts in which we made inquiries, 100 percent of eligible children had reportedly been immunized for most of the various diseases.

China apparently manufactures its own supply of all the vaccines used and thus avoids the problem common to most other developing countries—the prohibitively high cost of imported vaccines. It should also be noted that the full range of vaccines provided in China did not appear overnight. Today's program is said to be the result of gradual expansion, with polio and measles vaccines becoming available only in the late 1960s. Finally, it should also be mentioned that in almost every discussion of immunizations, someone, sooner or later, quoted Chairman Mao: "In health care, put the stress on prevention."

Health care in child-care facilities. The Chinese take advantage of the fact that many children are in educational institutions to provide both preventive services and primary care to the children enrolled. We often saw health-care personnel in full-time attendance in the schools we were shown. In the factories we saw, and in urban neighborhoods particularly, there was usually at least one full-time qualified physician, but the pattern varied. In some places, we met full-time barefoot doctors; in one, we met a teacher who had been selected, given six months of training, and then sent back to her school to be responsible for the health care in that school. In the larger schools, a team, usually consisting of two or three people, was responsible for health care. In some schools, teachers had been given short courses in health care.

Children are generally weighed and measured at regular intervals; immunizations are provided as called for in the immunization schedule; there is often a daily "health inspection," and primary treatment for acute illness is given as necessary. Schools where children were boarded invariably had small infirmaries, and we were told that children are isolated promptly when signs of infectious disease appear—reportedly an unusual event. In addition, the teachers, with the assistance of advisors from nearby health centers or municipal health offices, supervise school hygiene and the preparation of meals for the children.

Treatment of acute illness. Because of the network of health-care facilities, treatment for acute illness in infants and children is apparently easily come by, at least in the cities. Primary care for these illnesses is usually simple, but wherever detailed questioning was possible, it appeared that the health personnel on duty knew how to handle the problems commonly encountered, and were able to recognize those problems that needed to be referred to more sophisticated back-up facilities.

At almost every health facility visited, we were told in response to questions concerning the number of children who were brought in and the kinds of illnesses seen that very few children get sick anymore. A number of health workers responded that they are able to spend most of their time in disease prevention because they see so little acute illness. In the rural commune in Shensi province, we were told that a few children died of measles in the late 1950s, but that there have been no deaths in children under five since then. Similar stories were heard elsewhere. In school after school, health personnel could recall no deaths, or even hospital admissions, in recent years. In several of the larger health centers we visited, we were told that it is no longer necessary to provide outpatient clinics especially for infants and children because the demand has been so low in the last few years. At the Peking Children's Hospital, Dr. Wu Jui-ping showed Dr. Wray a fifteen-bed toddler's ward that has been "mothballed" because the number of children of that age admitted to the hospital these days is so low that it is not needed. Dr. Wu noted that in previous years this ward would have been full of children with pneumonia during late November, but that now such infections are treated promptly in health stations or health centers and only those children who have serious viral pneumonias need be admitted to the hospital.

Results. The combined effect of the total ecological situation in China, the antenatal and obstetric care provided to mothers, and the medical care, both preventive and curative, provided for children after birth, seems impressive, even though here, as always, truly satisfactory data are lacking. The most common indicator of the quality of such care is the infant mortality rate. Only estimates are available for China as a whole; they range from 17 per 1,000 live births to 30 per 1,000. Dr. Wu Jui-ping told us that infant mortality in Peking was 30 per 1,000 live births in 1965 and that it is now well below 20 per 1,000. The comparable rates for the United States in 1972 were 16.3 deaths per 1,000 live births in the white population, 29.0 per 1,000 in the non-white population.

Nutritional factors in child development

Breast feeding. In the cities and in the countryside of China today, breast feeding is reported to be still the "method of choice" for infant nutrition in the overwhelming majority of cases. Once again, no exact figures were available and, of course, no observations could be made, but the estimates of the proportion of children being breast fed were never less than 90 percent, and were more frequently on the order of 95 percent and occasionally even 100 percent. In the urban areas, the common practice is reportedly to continue breast feeding for eight or nine months; it is rarely continued beyond twelve months. In rural areas, on the other hand, babies are said to be breast fed for around eighteen months, and not infrequently for twenty-four months.

Given the devastating effect of maternal employment on breast feeding that has been observed in other parts of the world, the measures taken by the Chinese to facilitate breast feeding are worthy of note. Besides maternity leave, special provisions are often made to facilitate the continuation of breast feeding. In factories, as we noted earlier, infant nurseries or crèches are provided in some instances. In the rural communes, the work pattern is such that special provisions are not always necessary. Farmers traditionally rise at daybreak and go to the fields to work for a few hours. When the working fields are not too far away, they return to their homes for breakfast at about nine, then work for two or three more hours, until noon. Lunch is followed by a long rest period, especially during the hot summer months, and then another work period of approximately three hours in the late afternoon. Nursing mothers can thus, in some settings, breast feed their babies on awakening in the morning, when they return home for breakfast, at lunchtime, and after their late afternoon work period.

Artificial feeding. There are, of course, families in China today where the mother does not breast feed her infant. In these cases, either fresh milk or powdered milk is reportedly available. In no case, we were told, is it possible to provide such milk free. In China, as elsewhere, a cow's-milk substitute for human milk is rather expensive. In fact, the cost in China is reportedly approximately five U.S. dollars per month, and the entire diet in the second six months of life, where milk must be provided in addition to other foods, approximately ten U.S. dollars per month. This sum amounts to almost a fifth of the total cash income for a majority of the families. When we asked whether parents are indeed willing to spend such a large proportion of their income to feed an infant, we were assured that they are. Informants stressed the fact that the situation rarely arises because the overwhelming majority of mothers are able to breast feed their infants successfully.

Weaning and postweaning diets. Our limited time and occasional problems with translation also operated to constrain our observations here. Supplementary feeding was said to begin at around six months, rarely before that, and to consist initially of cereal-based porridges. Over the following months puréed vegetables, fruits, bean curd, and eggs are added. The exact sequence and ages reported varied from place to place and from informant to informant. Rice, noodles, and finally chopped meat—mainly chicken, pork, or fish—are added in the second year. Weaning is usually from breast to cup or small bowl. A "bean-flour milk," which is probably soybean based, was said to be frequently given. Children begin to feed themselves with a spoon in the second year; chopsticks are mastered at three or a bit later.

Meals at school. On several occasions we were able to visit kitchens in kindergartens, meet the staffs, and observe children consuming the food provided. Kitchen facilities were always clean and simple; food hygiene appeared to be excellent. Cooks wore white gowns and caps and seemed cheerful and competent. The weekly menu was posted on the kitchen wall in a few places and, as translated, seemed quite adequate. Menu planning, we were told, is supervised in all schools by the "child protection group" of the local health department, and the school's own health personnel. It is based, as institutional diets usually are, on carbohydrates—rice, noodles, steamed rolls, and so on—but included green and yellow vegetables, bean curd and other legumes, chopped meat of some kind or eggs daily or more frequently, fresh milk twice or three times weekly in some places, "bean-flour milk" regularly in others. At the season we visited, tangerines or apples were on the menu daily.

When we saw meals being consumed, the main dish was usually noodles or rice with substantial quantities of vegetables and either chopped meat, bean curd, or eggs on top. We were told that children are routinely provided "seconds" on request; they are encouraged to clean their bowls but not to eat too much. Chinese children, as we observed them, eat as they carry out many activities, with a quite remarkable, somehow cheerful concentration.

Growth and development

Children who are well nourished and relatively free from infection grow well, and for this reason, physical growth is one of the best indicators of the general health status of children. We were fortunate enough to come across growth data collected in 1967 on Shanghai children, and Dr. Wray collected height and weight measurements on children in four settings during our stay in China. We will discuss the observations shortly; they represent a contribution to the almost empty store of information about the growth of contemporary Chinese children. However, interpretation of the growth data is difficult for several reasons. First, there are no normative data on Chinese children, nor are there older Chinese data available to make estimates of change over time. Second, there is substantial regional variation in the size of Chinese and almost certainly variation related to nutrition; we have no way to estimate the typicality of our observations. Finally, we were not always certain of the precise ages of the children we saw. Nonetheless, we will try to provide a rough framework for the Chinese data by indicating how they compare with samples from other groups.

At each school we visited, Dr. Wray inquired about the possibility of obtaining height and weight measurements. Although we were assured that children are weighed and measured in all the schools, it was impossible to obtain data from many of them. More often than not, the reason given was that the records were elsewhere; in a few instances the responsible person was away, or the time was simply too short.

In four schools, heights and weights of children were available in school health records and were willingly provided. The numbers of records in each center ranged from 61 at Ren-min Street to 255 at Sian #1 Kindergarten, for a total of 553 altogether. Most of the children were between three and seven years of age. There is no way to know, of course, how carefully the children had been measured in each school. It was our impression that little use is made of the measurements; the children seem to be measured because measurement is part of the routine, rather than because of special or continuing interest.

With all of these qualifications in mind, it is readily apparent that the data we obtained can be taken only as an indication of the growth of the children in four schools in three cities. In Shanghai, however, there was at T'sao-yang what appeared to be a table of measurements, glassed and framed, hanging on the wall of the nursery-school doctor's office. Upon inquiry, we learned that the table presented the measurements obtained during an extensive survey of what was said to be a large, random sample of preschool children in Shanghai, carried out by municipal health authorities in 1967. Mean values and standard deviations for the measurements in each age group were calculated, the results tabulated, and the table was reproduced for circulation in Shanghai as a standard. Unfortunately, we were unable to learn more about the survey there or in subsequent conversations with physicians elsewhere in Shanghai. Still, the number of children measured in each age group, the care with which the tables had been prepared, and the consistency of the standard deviations combine to make this the most interesting set of data concerning the growth of Chinese children we were able to obtain.

Weights and heights in Shanghai, 1967. These data were reportedly obtained from measurements of 8,427 boys and 7,551 girls. For purposes of rough assessment, we compared the weights and heights with North American normative values and with reports on relatively large-scale anthropometric surveys of preschool children in Hong Kong (all Chinese) and Singapore (about three-quarters Chinese).

In brief summary, it appears that average weights and heights of all three Asian groups are equal to or greater than North American fiftieth-percentile levels in the first three months of life, then gradually fall to lower levels. Mean weights of Shanghai boys fall to the twenty-fifth-percentile level by the end of the first year of life, are slightly below it during the second and third years, and are slightly above that level during the rest of the preschool ages. Both Hong Kong and Singapore means fall to tenth-percentile levels by the end of the first year and remain below that level, with Singapore boys falling gradually to the third-percentile level by the sixth year. Mean heights of Shanghai boys remain above the twenty-fifth-percentile level throughout the preschool years, while the heights of Hong Kong boys remain at about that level and those of Singapore boys gradually decline to third-percentile levels. Growth in height among the Shanghai and Hong Kong boys thus more nearly approximates North American levels than does growth in weight.

In order to examine growth during the especially vulnerable period from six to twenty-four months more carefully, the Shanghai data on weight for the first two years of life were specifically compared with North American normative values and with corresponding data for a Hong Kong sample and two Bangkok samples, one of boys from middle-class families and one from squatter–slum-settlement families. It is clear that mean weights of boys from Shanghai and from the Bangkok middle-class families are well above North American seventy-fifth-percentile levels for the first three months, and decline toward the fiftieth percentile by the sixth month; Hong Kong boys are above the fiftieth at three months, well below it at six months. Shanghai boys fall to twenty-fifth-percentile levels by twelve months and remain at about that level throughout the remaining months of this period; the Bangkok middle-class boys, and those from Hong Kong, have fallen to near the tenth-percentile level by twelve months, and below that level thereafter, with the Bangkok boys falling below Hong Kong boys between eighteen and twenty-one months.

The Bangkok slum population includes a large proportion of infants who are not breast fed or who are weaned quite early. Their weight is only a little above the twenty-fifth percentile at three months, approaches the third percentile at six months, is below it by nine months, and remains well below that level thereafter.

Growth in Canton, Peking, and Sian, 1973. The height and weight data we obtained elsewhere in China are generally similar to the measurements obtained in Shanghai. In preparing these data for presentation here it was necessary to accept the age groupings, as given, in two of the schools. In these two schools, the mean weights and heights of the groups as given had been calculated. In the other two, where birth dates of the children were accessible, the age in months for each child at the time of the measurement was calculated, then the children grouped by six-month intervals, to calculate mean weights and heights. At the Renmin Street Nursery in Peking, birth dates were available for all the children present that day, and recent weights for most of them. Two members of the delegation measured the heights themselves.

Except for the children from Textile Mill #4 in Sian, where mean weights approximated North American fiftieth-percentile levels throughout, weights generally tended to be a bit lower than in Shanghai. Mean heights were generally between the North American twenty-fifth and fiftieth percentiles.

As a further indication of adequacy of individual growth, the percentile level for weight and height of each individual child was checked for all those for whom the age in months was known. In the nursery school in Peking, 44 percent of children under three years of age and 19 percent of those over three were above the North American fiftieth-percentile levels in weight, while 43 percent and 46 percent, respectively, were above those levels in height. For the total group, 8 percent and 2 percent were below third-percentile levels for height and weight, respectively. In Sian, in the under-three-years group 58 percent were over fiftieth-percentile levels for weight and 45 percent were above those levels for height. Among children over three, the proportion was similar for weight, but only 19 percent were above those levels for height. In the total group, 2 percent were below third-percentile levels for weight, 8 percent for height.

Overall assessment. Preschool children in China seem to be growing well, especially when compared to children in other developing countries. The evidence from the weight and height measurements confirms their general appearance of robust and vigorous good health. It might be noted that physical measurements must be accompanied by age data; not infrequently in developing countries, a child who appears to be a healthy four-year-old turns out to be six or seven years old. This seems not to be the case in China, at least in the schools where we were able to make measurements.

Several tentative conclusions can be drawn from the data presented here. Contemporary Chinese children demonstrate, in the early months of life, the potential to grow, both in height and in weight, as well as North American children. This is clear from the data from Shanghai, Hong Kong, and Singapore. Comparable data for this period of life were not obtained outside Shanghai; however, the fact that children elsewhere had heights and weights in the second year and later comparable to those in Shanghai suggests that they had grown equally well in the first year. The heights and weights of the small number of younger children in the Sian textile mill production are certainly consistent with such a conclusion.

The slowing of growth rates that commonly occurs in the latter half of the first year of life in developing countries also occurs in China, but neither height nor weight growth slow as markedly as is seen elsewhere. It seems particularly worth noting that the growth of the children of women factory workers, as reflected in the limited data from the Sian textile mill, seems to be excellent during this period. When these observations are compared with the growth of children of working mothers in Bangkok slums the difference is striking. Breast feeding in the early months, and the weaning diets given Chinese factory children, probably provide the nutrients required for better growth.

In the later preschool years, growth of the Chinese falls somewhat behind North American norms, but the average child is still well within "normal limits." If our limited observations are generalizable, children's growth throughout the preschool years suggests that they are receiving a basically adequate diet and that they are reasonably free of debilitating illnesses. Moreover, reported growth of children in Shanghai seems to be closer to North American standards than that of Chinese children in Hong Kong and Singapore.

Summary

Western students of child health have long been taught that children will thrive, and not merely survive, if a few simple requirements are met. Their mothers need a good diet during pregnancy and simple but competent antenatal and obstetric care; the children need a minimal but adequate diet—preferably human milk in the early months of life; they need a reasonably clean environment, with plenty of clean water; they need the basic immunizations against the common contagious diseases of childhood, administered properly, with potent vaccines; they need simple but prompt, inexpensive, and easily accessible treatment when they are ill, and the realistic possibility of rapid referral to more sophisticated facilities and personnel when necessary. They are better off if they are born into small families, with generous time intervals between the children. It is obvious that if families are to be small, and children well spaced, then parents must have access to family-planning services, and there must be a social climate that fully supports the utilization of those services.

The Chinese seem to be working hard to provide these conditions for children and their parents, at least in the largely urban settings we visited. The Chinese do not always measure up to their own or ideal standards, and by their own testimony, health services are not as well provided in all places as in some. Yet Chinese health care is outstanding, at least among developing countries, in the extent and the outreach of health activities and—judging by the health personnel we met—the enthusiasm, competence, commitment, and sense of responsibility of most health workers.

The peasants, or an urban facsimile thereof, celebrate a bountiful harvest and the joy of sending a share to their fellow countrymen.

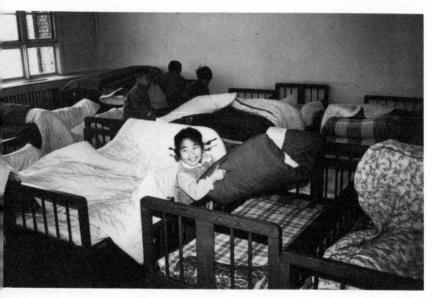

After awakening from an afternoon nap, nursery children dress and make their beds. The routines seem natural and unquestioned.

We were sometimes greeted with enthusiasm, sometimes with restraint, almost never with withdrawal or fear. The caps are replicas of those worn by the soldiers of the People's Liberation Army.

While adults gather outside the fence to watch the American visitors, kindergarten children go on with their games, an image of shared order and busy activity.

9. *LOOKING BACK*

In retrospect, we know more than we have told about childhood in China and we know far less than we want to. The omissions in our record are less significant than our ignorance; they represent largely the failure of a narrative account to catch the concrete and particular detail of life in the streets and schools of China. In our memories as in our photographs, there are images that carry meanings difficult to lay out in a balanced prose statement. To take just a few examples, we can only hint at the social expressivity of four- and five-year-old Chinese children, we cannot document the slow and steady evolution of drab standard adult clothing from the wildly colorful and varying clothing of infants and young children, we cannot represent dramatically enough the dusty cleanliness of the cities and the villages, we cannot properly describe the sight and sound of thousands of bicycles moving through Kwangchow, and, ultimately, we cannot tell one unified story of our personal engagement with and interpretation of what we saw of China, because the members of the delegation varied radically from one another in their interpretation of what they saw.

The limited nature of our knowledge about Chinese children is of greater concern than our limited ability to communicate what we do know and feel. There are several reasons for guarding our generalizations and the reasons are different enough to justify a word about each of them before risking a concluding statement.

The first limitations on our information were, as we have noted before, the brevity of our visit and the inability of most of us to speak and to understand Chinese. Moreover, clearly we were honored foreign guests on tour; we saw many schools for just a few hours, we rarely saw schools that no earlier foreign visitors had seen (and where children and teachers were not familiar with

215

visitors), and, with few exceptions, we were in large cities and their suburbs. Even more critically, however, and modifying our observations even in those instances when we were able to stay long enough in a kindergarten or school to deepen our understanding of it, our interaction with Chinese children and teachers always fell under the ancient and rather narrowly prescribed definition of guest–host, visitor–visited social contact. Throughout the trip, we longed to penetrate the work of education rather than only stand nearby it. We learned for ourselves what is a commonplace for anthropologists, that an unknown distance separates the private from the public in someone else's culture.

But the fundamental limitation on our observations rests on the fact that, in China as in all other nations, the exchange between parent and child, between teacher and student, is rooted in the larger context of the culture. Chinese schools and, in a profound way that unnerved us a bit, Chinese children are defined by a long history of the culture's respect for order, restraint, deference to authority, and for service to the group above individual achievement. Thus, comparisons between individual fragments of our observations and specific Western ways would not be valid. Nor can we in this limited sphere address the question so often posed since our return: what implications can be drawn for American parents and American schools from observations in contemporary China? We have had to be content with describing what we saw as carefully as we can, in full recognition that we brought to our description not only eyes and ears and notebooks, but our own ideological and culture-limited ways of seeing and hearing and understanding.

A paradox, a proposition, and two puzzles

If our observations were at all representative, the outstanding feature of childhood in China, and that which raises the most basic problem, is the high level of concentration, orderliness, and competence of the children. We were impressed by the sight of fifty children in a primary classroom quiet until addressed and chanting their lessons in enthusiastic unison when called upon, even more impressed by the apparent absence of disruptive, hyperactive, and noisy children. The same quiet orderliness, the same concentration on tasks, the same absence of disruptive behavior was to be seen in all the classrooms we visited, down to children barely able to walk. The docility did not seem to us to be the docility of surrender and apathy; the Chinese children we saw were emotionally expressive, socially gracious, and adept.

We talked a great deal to teachers about the control and restraint of children; we inquired about hyperactive and aggressive behavior; we tried, not very successfully, to describe some of the behavior problems in American schools. By and large, Chinese teachers did not understand what we were talking about; they had never seen a hyperactive or disruptive child in school. Some children were occasionally "lively" or "naughty," but apparently not for long.

The problem, then, is to account for this conspicuously prosocial behavior. With the sense of our limitations expressed above, we want to present some preliminary formulations of factors we believe will figure in a solution.

STABILITY IN THE LIVES OF CHILDREN: A PARADOX.   The most commonly held image of contemporary China is of significant, even unsettling, change: from the transformation of 1949 to the Cultural Revolution, China has been in transition and turmoil. But, and herein lies the paradox, we suspect that the young Chinese child grows up in the presence of remarkable stability.

Earlier on, we mentioned cultural continuities in Chinese life that may give a stable ground for educational practice, and it is surely the case that Chinese classrooms in Canton, Taipai, San Francisco, and New York (at least until the last decade or so) show noteworthy similarities. But the stability of life for children in contemporary China has more mundane representations. It is difficult for Americans of our mobile time to recognize that most Chinese, urban and rural, live their lives in continuous and enduring neighborhoods, knowing both the spaces and the people of the environment. In ways that warrant further study, Chinese children (like the children of traditional cultures generally) know the details of their surroundings very well indeed and can have high expectations that they will remain pretty much the same throughout childhood. Networks of sociability, power, and caretaking are apparently clear. Even the minor dislocations of the students' annual work time in the country do not violate the traditional patterns of family cohesiveness over distance. We cannot, however, say how the sending down of educated youth will affect this sense of stability; it does seem to us to be a more wrenching change.

Most visible of all is the stability of the commitment to national development. The Chinese—at least those with whom we came in contact—seem dedicated to a unified society based on Mao Tsetung's reading of Communist ideology. The variations of politics have had an important disorganizing impact on university education and the life of middle schools, but one may guess that, for children short of adolescence, the stability of the national commitment supports and reflects the older stabilities of Chinese culture.

The apparent stability which is of great interest to developmental psychologists, but which is the most difficult to study and to document, is the stable expectation Chinese adults have about what a child is and what he can become. Amidst all the variety of circumstances and ages, we had no sense that Chinese parents and teachers were conflicted about the goals of education and child rearing in the formation of personality. Once more in a way surprising to Americans tuned to fads, experts, and advice columns in newspapers, Chinese adults appeared to share, almost without exception, a conception of what a properly raised child should be like.

This stability, if it truly exists, sets the stage for significant changes in the lives of Chinese children. If the cultural sharing is weakened, if the parallelism between classical child-rearing and educational procedures on one hand and ideological expectations on the other is diminished—and we must think of the major attack on stability presented by the sending down of youth—then China, like other modernizing societies, will be required to build a new conception of what it means to be a child in Chinese society.

PRACTICAL EXPECTATIONS: A PROPOSITION.   Over and over we asked ourselves how the very young Chinese child was brought to competence, social grace, and restraint. It did little good to ask Chinese adults about the problem, for two important reasons. For one, there was little professional interest in examining or discussing potential sources of variation in children and, as might be expected from the presence of a shared conception of children, there was little interest in the problem of variety as we were posing it. Everyone could join us in talking about sex differences, and differences as a result of variation in early schooling, and so on, but we could arouse little enthusiasm for talking about our first question—how do Chinese children come to be as they are? Therein lies a message, perhaps reflecting the relative lack of cosmopolitan perspectives on other cultures among Chinese adults, about the pragmatic attitude of high and stable expectations for children among Chinese adults. Put in its most simplifying form, Chinese children behave the way they do because *that is the way* children behave! The contrast with common American practice can be easily made. An American teacher (or parent) considers how he or she will effect a change in a child, what *should be done* with the child to make a difference. This attitude, which runs across many different theories of education, sees teaching as instrumental, as a set of procedures for the purpose of changing behavior. If the instruments of education, whether they are problem setting, positive reinforcement, or modeling, are ineffective, then change is difficult or distorted. Such a consciously instrumental attitude seems far less prevalent in Chinese schools. Rather, we formed the impression that Chinese teachers have uniform expectations of what children at one or another age can do and that they behave with the virtually certain knowledge that the children would come to behave in the expected way—and, critically, it did not much matter whether the children got there early or late. The

stance of Chinese parents and teachers, then, is not so much systematically and consciously instrumental as, in an unpolitical way,
ideological. Normal development is a process in which both adults
and children participate, with relatively little doubt about or analysis of the goals to be reached. The adults know what a child
should be like, they behave as though it were certain the child
would behave in the expected way; and on his side the child joins
a social structure where the definition of his place and the definition of his proper behavior are, by and large, without ambiguity
and without conflict. Apparently, under these circumstances, the
ideology of expectations often becomes the fact of child behavior.

We could not, in the short time we had, pursue the implications
of the proposition that education of the very young in China is
accommodation to high and highly shared adult expectations and
we must leave our proposition as hypothesis. Nonetheless, we
were struck by the generally nonanalytic (educational theorists
might even say "unscientific") posture of Chinese teachers toward
their children. There seemed no commanding need either for
theories of classroom "management" or, let it be emphasized, for
theories of child development.

THE ACQUISITION OF SKILLS AND THE MANAGEMENT OF
CONFLICT: TWO PUZZLES. We close our report on Chinese
children with two questions for further study—not the only ones
or even the most important ones but, certainly beguiling ones.
How do children learn the remarkably precise and by American
standards advanced forms of dance, sculpture, and music? And
how do Chinese parents and teachers manage the first signs of
conflict among young children? We cannot even make a wise
guess about the answers to either question; we can only testify, as
others have done, to the skilfulness of five-year-old Chinese in the
performance of dance routines of memorable complexity and to
the ability of such children to prepare, almost always from an
established model, exact and convincing paintings and sculptures.
When we watched young children learn a new song and recognized
the ease with which they did so, we were persuaded that Chinese

teachers had developed procedures for early education in the domains of dance and figural representation that would be profitable for us to understand.

The puzzle of conflict—how social restraint and amity are achieved so early and so generally—is more difficult to specify and will undoubtedly be more difficult to study. The orderliness of Chinese classsrooms, to say nothing of the streets and the parks and the factory dormitories, forces American students of children to ask how such order is established and maintained, and at what cost to individual variety and creativity. We cannot hazard a guess, but we left China convinced that we had seen radically different ways of thinking about and meeting children from the ways we knew as Americans. It will take many more, and more concentrated, observations of children as they grow up in the two societies before we can move from speculation and hypothesis to principles defining the interplay of culture and the development of young children.

APPENDIX: NOTE ON PEOPLE AND PLACES

The members of the American Delegation on Early Childhood Development were:

William Kessen, Professor of Psychology, Yale University

Urie Bronfenbrenner, Professor of Human Development and Family Studies and Psychology, Cornell University

Bettye Caldwell, Professor of Elementary Education, University of Arkansas

John A. Clausen, Professor of Sociology, University of California at Berkeley

Alex de Angelis, Professional Associate, Committee on Scholarly Communication with the People's Republic of China, National Academy of Sciences

Jerome Kagan, Professor of Human Development, Harvard University

Eleanor E. Maccoby, Professor of Developmental Psychology, Stanford University

George A. Miller, Professor, The Rockefeller University

Harold W. Stevenson, Professor of Psychology, University of Michigan

Jeannette G. Stone, Director, Early Childhood Center, Sarah Lawrence College

Martin K. Whyte, Assistant Professor of Sociology and Associate of the Center for Chinese Studies, University of Michigan

Joe Wray, Field Staff, Health Services, The Rockefeller Foundation

Marian Radke Yarrow, Chief, Laboratory of Developmental Psychology, National Institute of Mental Health

ITINERARY AND LIST OF PEOPLE MET IN CHINA

The names of the people we met appear in alphabetical order for each occasion. The names of persons met for the first time appear in capitals and precede those of persons met earlier. Formal activities such as banquets and discussions, with the names of the persons present, are included in chronological order. Sightseeing visits are mentioned only in notes under each geographical heading. Mr. Hsieh Ch'i-kang and Mr. Hao Shuang-hsing were with us at nearly all times, therefore, their names are mentioned only on the first occurrence and at formal activities.

All names were identified aurally; with the press of people and activities during the visit, it was impossible to be certain that we had a complete and fully accurate list. We apologize to our Chinese hosts for any inaccuracies and omissions in our lists.

KWANGCHOW (CANTON)

Sightseeing visits included White Cloud Mountain and a tour of the city.

NOVEMBER 15

MR. CHU CHIN-LIU	Kwangchow City Education Bureau
MS. CHU TAO-MIN	Interpreter, Kwangchow City Education Bureau
MR. HAO SHUANG-HSING	Middle and primary school group of the Peking City Education Bureau
MR. HSIEH CH'I-KANG	Foreign Relations section of the Group on Science and Education under the State Council
MR. HSU WEN-FENG	Principal of Kwangchow city schools
LIN SHOU-CHIH	Kwangchow City Education Bureau
MR. LU CHAN-MING	Responsible person for primary education in the Kwangchow

	City Education Bureau
MS. SUNG YUEH-TS'UNG	Kindergarten section of the Kwangchow City Education Bureau
MR. WANG CHIN-SHAN	Interpreter (Kwangchow Foreign Language Institute?)

Dinner at Pan-hsi Restaurant

MR. CHANG YEN	Kwangchow City Education Bureau

Mr. Chu Chin-liu
Mr. Hao Shuang-hsing
Mr. Hsieh Ch'i-kang
Mr. Hsu Weng-feng
Lin Shou-chih
Mr. Lu Chan-ming
Ms. Sung Yueh-ts'ung
Mr. Wang Chin-shan

NOVEMBER 16

East-Is-Red Kindergarten and Chao-yang Kindergarten of the Hsin-chiao People's Commune

MS. MA	Director of the leadership group of Chao-yang Kindergarten, Red Guard Brigade, Hsin-chiao Commune
MS. T'AN P'ENG-HUNG	Principal of the East-Is-Red Kindergarten of the Tung-shan District
MS. TSENG WEI-GUNG	Kwangchow City Education Bureau

Ms. Chang Yen
Lin Shou-chih

NOVEMBER 17

Kwangchow Heavy Machinery Factory Kindergarten and Nursery

MS. CH'EN	In charge of Kwangchow Heavy Machinery Factory Kindergarten

MR. LU   Secretary of the Revolutionary
                                Committee of the Factory

Flight to Peking

PEKING

NOVEMBER 17

Sightseeing included T'ien-an-men Square, the Great Wall, Ming Tombs, Temple of Heaven, and the Peking Friendship Store.

MR. CHAO WEI-LI   Responsible Person in the Peking
                             City Education Bureau
MS. CHU CHUEH   Interpreter, English department of
                             Peking Foreign Language
                             Institute
MR. HSU TZU-KUANG   Interpreter
MR. HUANG NAI-K'UN   Person in charge of middle and
                             primary schools in the Peking
                             City Education Bureau

NOVEMBER 18

Reception

MS. CH'EN CHUN-T'IEN

MS. CHI KUEI-HUA   Kindergarten education, Peking
                             City Education Bureau
MR. FENG KUEI-HSI   Foreign affairs section of Group
                             on Science and Education
                             under the State Council
MR. HSIAO CHING-JO   Head of the primary and middle
                             school education section of the
                             Group on Science and
                             Education under the State
                             Council
MS. HSIEH MING   Responsible person in charge of
                             Capital Iron and Steel Mill
                             Kindergarten

HSU FU-KUANG

MR. HSU YUN-PEI — Vice-chairman of the Peking City Revolutionary Committee

MR. LI CH'EN — Peking City Revolutionary Committee

LING HAO-HSING
Mr. Chao Wei-li
Mr. Feng Kuei-hsi
Mr. Hsieh Ch'i-kang
Mr. Hsu Tzu-kuang
Mr. Huang Nai-k'un

NOVEMBER 19

Capital Iron and Steel Kindergarten and Kindergarten #5

MS. CHANG — Director of Kindergarten #5 of the Kuang-ming Road of the Ch'ung-wen District

CHIAO YU-CHIN — Responsible person for Kindergarten #5

HUANG WEI-CH'EN — Vice-director of Kindergarten #5

MR. KAO — Head of the general office of the Revolutionary Committee of Capital Iron and Steel

NOVEMBER 20

Ta-an lan-ying Kindergarten and Peking Cotton Mill Kindergarten #3

MS. HSI — Responsible person for Cotton Mill Kindergarten

MR. NAN PEI-HO — Responsible person in charge of Peking Cotton Mill #3

MS. SUN — Director of the Ta-an lan-ying Kindergarten of the Hsuan-wu District of Peking

NOVEMBER 21

Sightseeing

NOVEMBER 22

(Split into three sub-groups)

*Peking Middle School #31, Hsin-hua Primary #2,
Jen-min Street Nursery*

MS. CHANG YU-JU	Responsible person of educational reform group of Peking Middle School #31
MR. FAN	Chairman of the Revolutionary Committee of #31
MR. HSU CHA	Vice-secretary of the Youth League (Mao Tse-tung Thought Propaganda Team) at #31
MR. JEN CH'I-SHU	Responsible person for #31 school factory
MS. MA WEN-CHUN	Vice-chairman of the Revolutionary Committee of Peking Middle School #31
MS. PAO CHEN	Teacher
MR. TING	Chairman of the Revolutionary Committee of Hsin-hua Primary School #2

Night Meeting with Leaders of Education in Peking

MR. WU	Medical doctor and vice-chairman of the Revolutionary Committee of Children's Hospital and head of the Peking Child Health Center
MS. CHAO	Psychologist with Chinese Academy of Sciences

Ms. Chang Yu-ju
Mr. Chao Wei-li
Ms. Ch'en Chun-t'ien
Ms. Chi Kuei-hua
Ms. Chu Chueh
Mr. Fan
Mr. Feng Kuei-hsi
Mr. Hao Shuang-hsing

Mr. Hsiao Ching-jo
Mr. Hsieh Ch'i-kang
Ms. Hsieh Ming
Mr. Hsu Tzu-kuang
Mr. Huang Nai-k'un
Ms. Ma Wen-chun
Mr. Ting

NOVEMBER 23

(Split into three groups)

Hsin-hua Primary #2, Peking Middle #31 and Pei-hai Kindergarten

NOVEMBER 24

Dinner given by the Delegation for our Hosts

Mr. Chao Wei-li
Ms. Ch'en Chun-t'ien
Ms. Chi Kuei-hua
Ms. Chu Chueh
Mr. Feng Kui-hsi
Mr. Hao Shuang-hsing
Mr. Hsiao Ching-jo
Mr. Hsieh Ch'i-kang
Mr. Hsu Tzu-kuang
Mr. Hsu Yun-pei
Mr. Huang Nai-k'un
Mr. Li Ch'en

NOVEMBER 25

Flight to Sian

SIAN

Sightseeing included Pan-p'o Neolithic village, Sian City Museum, the Big Goose Pagoda, and Hua-Ch'ing Hot Springs.

NOVEMBER 25

MR. CHANG TA-LIANG   Staff member of Shensi Province

	Foreign Affairs Bureau
CHI FU-YUNG	Shensi Province Foreign Affairs Bureau
MR. CHIANG CH'ANG-CHU	Director of Shensi Province Foreign Affairs Bureau
MS. CH'IN YU-YIN	Interpreter from the Sian City Foreign Language Institute
MS. FANG LI	Responsible Person for Sian City Education Bureau
MR. PAI	Staff Member of the Shensi Province Foreign Affairs Bureau
MS. PAI T'IEN-HUI	Sian City Education Bureau
MR. PAI YU-FENG	Responsible member for Shensi Province Foreign Affairs Bureau
MR. TU JUI-CH'ING	Interpreter from the Sian City Foreign Language Institute

NOVEMBER 26

Feng-huo Production Brigade Kindergarten and Primary School, Feng-huo People's Commune, Sian

MR. WANG HSING	Vice-chairman of the Revolutionary Committee of Feng-huo Production Brigade

NOVEMBER 27

Ch'ang-an Junior and Senior Middle School and Textile Plant #4, Northwest

NOVEMBER 28

Sian Kindergarten #1

MS. CHIN	Director of Kindergarten #1
MS. FANG	Revolutionary Committee of Kindergarten #1
MS. LING	Vice-director of Sian Kindergarten #1

NOVEMBER 28

Reception

Mr. Chang Ta-liang
Chi Fu-yung
Mr. Chiang Ch'ang-chu
Ms. Ch'in Yu-yin
Ms. Fang Li
Mr. Hao Shuang-hsing
Mr. Hsieh Ch'i-kang
Ms. Pai T'ien-hui
Mr. Pai Yu-feng
Mr. Tu Jui-ch'ing

NOVEMBER 29

Shang-te Road Primary School, Sian

MR. T'ANG FU   Responsible member for School

Flight to Shanghai

SHANGHAI

Sightseeing included the Shanghai Youth Palace, the Industrial Exhibit, and the Shanghai Friendship Store.

NOVEMBER 29

Briefing

MS. CH'EN YING-FEI	Interpreter, Shanghai Foreign Language Institute
MS. CHOU FU-YING	Interpreter, Shanghai Foreign Language Institute
HSUEH HAO-MING	Interpreter, Shanghai Foreign Language Institute
MS. HUA CHIN-MEI	Person in charge of middle and primary school education
MS. LI HUA-MEI	Person in charge of kindergarten education in the Shanghai City Education Bureau

MS. LI LI   Responsible person of the
                                    Shanghai City Education
                                    Bureau and Member of the
                                    Revolutionary Committee of
                                    the board of education

MS. LIN CH'I-CHANG   Staff member of the board of
                                    education

MS. LIU FANG   Chairman of the Revolutionary
                                    Committee of the Shanghai
                                    City Education Bureau

MR. SUN PAO-CH'ENG   Staff member of the board of
                                    education

NOVEMBER 30

Feng-sen Workers' Village of the Yang-p'u District,
    primary school

MR. KU LUNG   Leader of the Street
                                    Revolutionary Committee

LU HSU-CH'EN   Member of the Revolutionary
                                    Committee of the Street,
                                    Yang-p'u District

Ms. Ch'en Ying-fei
Ms. Chou Fu-ying
Hsueh Hao-ming
Ms. Li Li
Ms. Lin Ch'i-chang
Mr. Sun Pao-ch'eng

DECEMBER 1

T'sao-yang Workers' Village neighborhood nursery and
    kindergarten and the Shanghai Experimental Primary School

CHANG   Teacher at the Shanghai
                                    Experimental Primary School

MS. CHANG TZU-LING   Person in charge of kindergarten
                                    from the Revolutionary
                                    Committee of the street of the
                                    Ts'ao-yang Workers' Village

MR. WEI   Work master at the Shanghai
                                Experimental Primary School

Reception

Ms. Ch'en Ying-fei
Ms. Chou Fu-ying
Mr. Hao Shuang-hsing
Mr. Hsieh Ch'i-kang
Hsueh Hao-ming
Ms. Hua Chin-yu
Ms. Li Hua-mei
Ms. Li Li
Ms. Lin Ch'i-chang
Ms. Liu Fang
Mr. Sun Pao-ch'eng

DECEMBER 2

Discussions in Hotel

MS. CHANG   Doctor at International Peace
                                   Maternity Hospital #32
MS. CH'EN   Pediatrician
FAN   Pediatrician and family-planning
                                   worker
HUNG TU-HO   Psychologist from normal school
LI TAN   Psychologist from normal school
LIU
MEI CHIA-HUA   Psychologist from normal school
TSO PEI-LI   Psychologist from normal school

DECEMBER 3

July First People's Commune Kindergarten and Nursery

CHANG FU-LING   Education administration worker
JUI HSIAO-SHA   Administrative office of the
                                   Revolutionary Committee of
                                   commune
LIN HSIANG   Staff member of the
                                   Revolutionary Committee

YANG CHI-HUA   Education administration worker
YU HSING-YIN   Person in charge of kindergarten
                                work

DECEMBER 4

Shanghai Primary #2

DECEMBER 5

   Fly back to Kwangchow

   Leave for Hong Kong

INDEX

INDEX

American Delegation on Early Childhood Development: study range of, *x–xiii*; members of, *xi*, 225; evaluation of limitations of observations, 215–16; evaluation of prosocial behavior, 216–21; itinerary of, and people met by, 226–36

Bangkok: weight and height statistics for children in, 209, 211

Canton (Kwangchow): nursery school visited in, 54, 75; kindergarten visited in, 73, 75, 81, 85, 102
Capital Hospital (Peking), 187, 189, 200
Capital Iron and Steel Factory Nursery School (Peking), 53
Chang, Doctor, 195
Chang Yu-ju: on Revolutionary Committees, 10
Cheng, Doctor, 195
Children's Hospital (Peking), 187, 203–04
Committee on Planned Birth Work, 194
Committee on Scholarly Communication with the People's Republic of China, *x, xi*

Determinism, environmental, 5–7
Dieny, J. P.: *Le monde est à vous: la Chine et les livres pour enfants*, 126n1

East-Is-Red Kindergarten (Canton), 73, 81, 102

Family life: role of grandparent in child care, 2, 35–37, 45; other agents in child care, 2, 37–38; evaluation of observations made of, 15–16, 50; country vs. city, 17–23, 198; vignettes of, 23–35; role of parents in, 37, 42; Maoist line related to, 38; child behavior and child-rearing practices, 38–41; parent–teacher relationship, 43–47; supports and constraints for, 47–49; health and planning programs for, 193–201; child development related to stability of, 217–20
Fan, Doctor, 195
Feng-huo People's Commune (Sian), *xii*, 15, 17–18

Grant, John, 189
Great Leap Forward (*1958–60*), 3
Group on Science and Education of the State Council, *x*, 8

Hao Shuang-hsing, *x*
Health care: health workers, 46–48 passim, 190–91, 193–97 passim, 199, 201; in schools, 56, 111, 190, 202–03, 206; housing and sanitation, 188; diet, 188; ideology of, 188–89, 193, 197; decentralization of, 189–90; neighborhood units for, 191, 194, 199, 201, 202; back-up facilities for, 191–92; cost of, 192–93; family-planning program, 193–97; maternal-health programs, 197–200; premarital

237